Canada's Daughter

The Story of Captain Nichola Goddard

Canada's Daughter

The Story of Captain Nichola Goddard

Sally Goddard

Underhill Books

ISBN: 978-0-9950270-7-7

First published by Underhill Books in 2017.

Underhill Books
4183 Murray Harbour Road
RR#3 Belfast PE C0A 1A0

THIS BOOK IS DEDICATED TO
EVERYONE WHO KNEW HER,
AND THOSE WHO WISHED THEY HAD

Contents

Acknowledgements

Acknowledgements

I would like to thank the staff and students of the Captain Nichola Goddard School in Calgary, Alberta for their willingness to constructively criticize the manuscript. I would particularly like to thank the founding principal of the school, Dr. Joy Chadwick, who encouraged and supported the process.

Thank you also to Jaime Phillips for writing such a wonderful introduction, and to Krista and Jay. Krista said reading it was like sitting around the dining room table at dinner listening to stories.

I would also like to thank Linda Granfield, whom I first met in Charlottetown several years ago and who encouraged me to complete this book; and Lisa LaFlamme, who has done more than she will ever know to help keep Nichola's memory alive for Tim and me.

Finally, my deepest thanks to Victoria, who brought the book to life; to Kate and Andrew, who provided support and encouragement; and to Tim, without whom there would be no story.

Preface

Preface

Nichola was exceptional.

I think she would have disliked my use of the term, but I stand by my decision. When I found out she had been killed in Afghanistan my first thought was: "Well, if they got Nichola, there is *literally* no hope for the rest of us."

She was the best at what she did, as both a leader and a soldier. She never took shortcuts. She never shied away from hard work, and if she saw something that needed fixing, she fixed it. She brought out the best in everyone around her, and somehow simultaneously made them feel as though in the end, no matter what happened, everything would be alright. For her then to NOT be alright was unfathomable to me.

I met her when I was 17 years old, and I knew immediately that she was special. I had recently graduated high school as well as the army cadet program, and although I was lucky to have had many exceptional female leaders and teachers in my life, at that point the

Disney movie *Mulan* was pretty much all I knew of women in war (try not to laugh ...). Nichola, however, had already completed artillery officer training, and she was one of the third years who was in charge of us first years when we arrived at the Royal Military College in the year 2000. She was fit, formidable, and authoritative. I was in awe of her. But she was also brilliant, compassionate, and human. She was all of us.

This book is about what shaped her into the exceptional person and leader that she was. It's a great story, and well-told. May she live on through the words written about her, and through the enduring love of her friends, family, and soldiers.

—Major Jaime Phillips, MMM, CD
Royal Regiment of Canadian Artillery

Introduction

Introduction

On Friday May 26, 2006, my daughter Nichola's funeral was held at St Barnabas Anglican Church in Calgary. She was killed in Afghanistan on May 17, the first Canadian female soldier to die in combat and the first Canadian officer to be killed in Afghanistan. The funeral was very public and well-attended.

One of the television commentators said, "She was a 26-year-old in a position of authority leading men, breaking down barriers, having to deal with it in a country where women are not seen in the same role as they are seen here in the Western world, and being cited for doing such a tremendous job."

In the years that have followed, her father and I have often been asked why we let her join the military, and why we let her go to Afghanistan. We try to explain that it was not our decision, that once your child reaches the age of 18, your job as a parent is done. Your children may ask your opinion, but they make their own decisions.

When I finished university in 1974, I accepted a two-year teaching assignment with CUSO (Canadian University Services Overseas) in Papua New Guinea. In January 1976, Tim Goddard arrived from England and ended up teaching at the same school. We married in 1977 in Alotau, Milne Bay Province, Papua New Guinea. We ended up staying in Papua New Guinea until December 1983.

As I have put together Nichola's story, I realize that inadvertently, we prepared her for Afghanistan. She was born in Papua New Guinea, and spent her first four years there, living in remote villages and eating different food. When we came to Canada in February 1984, we lived in northern Canada for almost 10 years, living in remote communities and eating 'country food'. In Afghanistan, some of the village people were surprised that she would eat their food. We weren't.

Before Nichola joined the military, she had gone to eight schools in seven different communities in five different provinces and one territory. Nichola always liked order in her life and the military provided that. Tim and I gave her a childhood like no other. It was anything other than orderly. This is that story.

Sally Goddard
Charlottetown

Papua New Guinea

1979 – 1984

When I found out I was pregnant with Nichola, we were living at Passam National High School, about 30 km outside of Wewak in the northwest corner of Papua New Guinea.

I was teaching Grade 11 English and History. Tim was head of the Expressive Arts Department and taught a variety of art forms to Grade 11 and Grade 12 students. My father turned 60 in November 1979, and we decided that we would telephone him and tell him his first grandchild was on the way, due sometime in May.

Tim and I didn't have a telephone. We could use the two-way radio in the school office but first we had to figure out what time and day it was in Canada. Eventually, after much discussion and arithmetic, we thought that if we called in the late afternoon on the 14th of November, it would be breakfast time, the morning of my father's birthday, in Sault Ste Marie, Ontario.

We called the operator and gave him the phone number. But we couldn't just say we'd like to call Canada (705) 2530713. We had to use the phonetic alphabet so the operator could understand the number.

Today, very few people use a telephone operator, but in 1979, if you wanted to call outside of the country, you had to dial 0 for the operator. The school had a two-way telephone so you had to say "over" every time you finished a sentence.

I said, "I'd like to call Canada, please. Over."

The operator said, "How do you spell that? Over."

I said, "C for Charlie, A for Alpha, N for November, A for Alpha, D for Delta, A for alpha. Over."

The operator said, "Ah, Canada. What number please? Over."

I then gave the operator the number, and eventually, we were connected. My father answered the phone.

He said, "Hello."

However, he didn't know about saying 'over'.

I said, "Dad, it's me, Sally. Over."

He said immediately, "Is there anything wrong?"

I said, "You have to say 'over' when you have finished talking and are waiting for a reply. Over."

My father said, "I haven't done that since the war. Over."

So I wished him a happy birthday and told him the good news. He asked, "When's the baby due? Over."

I responded, "Sometime towards the end of May, the beginning of June. Over."

He then asked where I was going to have the baby. I hadn't really thought about that. I said, "I guess I will have it here. People have babies here all the time. It should be fine. Over."

We didn't talk for long. My father was pleased with the news but concerned about health care facilities. Later, he wrote and said, "Ninety percent of the time it doesn't matter where you have the baby. It will be born. But 10 percent of the time you need to be close to a hospital." I was young and healthy. I was sure nothing would go wrong.

During my first and second trimester, I visited the prenatal clinic in Wewak monthly. It was about 20 km on a dirt road that often could only be accessed by a 4-wheel drive vehicle. By my third trimester, the clinic was worried that I wasn't putting on enough weight. I was instructed only to teach, not to participate in any other activities. Teachers were expected to work three afternoons a week supervising work parade.

I had started a poultry project the year before and we now provided eggs and chicken for the kitchen. I worried about the chickens and in the afternoon as I put my feet up, I could watch the students and another teacher. The view was fabulous from our porch. You could see the school buildings and the chicken house across the small valley.

One morning I woke up, hearing all kinds of squawking. I shook Tim. "Someone is trying to break into the chicken house. Please go and find out what's happening."

It was light, so it must have been after 6 a.m. Tim pulled on his shorts and his rubber boots, grabbed a bush knife (machete) and headed off.

When he returned, he said, "I opened the door to the pen. To begin with all I could see was chickens flying all over the place. Then I looked again. There was a huge python having his breakfast. I told him to help himself. I wasn't about to stop him."

Tim could see three clear bumps in the snake so we had lost at least three chickens. He mentioned that a couple of the students were tracking the snake. They were big Grade 12 boys that I had worked with for two years.

When we got down to school for classes, the boys found Tim and told him they had killed the snake and three of them had carried it down to the school. Tim went over to see it. It was 6 metres long with 3 bumps, one for each chicken it had eaten. When I went to go and see it, the boys stopped me. In my condition, they said, it would be bad for the baby. So I never did see it but I have imagined it for a long time.

In those days, a woman would get 6 weeks off when she was pregnant. You could take time off before the birth and then subtract it from the time off after. I decided to work until the end of the term, and then take the following six weeks off. On Monday, April 29th. I drove down to Wewak for my weekly prenatal checkup. The doctor was concerned that the baby was in the wrong position. There was no ultra-sound so he did an x-ray. It confirmed that the baby was not going to come out easily.

The doctor was worried about complications and felt that I needed to see a specialist. The closest one was in Madang, about an hour's flying time away. Tim and I wanted to delay the trip. We didn't think the baby was due until the end of May. My mother was arriving on May 24th. However, the medical people convinced us that time was of the essence. The health department provided us with plane tickets but we were on our own for accommodation and food.

We arrived at the Wewak airport on Tuesday, April 30th. The plane was in but there were no seats available, even though we had tickets. There was a Japanese tour group waiting to board the plane. Wewak had been the site of the largest Japanese airbase in New Guinea during World War II so it was on the tourist route for many Japanese people.

The airline agent was an ex-student of ours and he stopped one Japanese couple from getting on the plane so Tim and I could have seats. The couple was promised seats on the next flight and a free lunch.

What we didn't know was that the airline was expecting a strike later on that day. The plane we left on was the last one to arrive in Wewak for five days. I have always wondered about what might have happened if we had missed that flight. I also wonder what happened to the tourists.

We arrived in Madang, rented a car, and found a hotel room. The hotel was right on the water and a little extravagant but it would only be for a day or two. Our appointment with the specialist was not until the next day and we decided to be tourists.

We went to the Coastwatchers' Tower, a memorial built to those Australians and Papua New Guineans who lost their lives sending radio messages about Japanese movements during World

War II. We ended our afternoon at the Madang Teachers' College where several of our graduating students had gone. It was wonderful to see them settled and happy with their career choices.

When we returned to the hotel, we discovered that the airline that had bought us to Madang was now on strike. We weren't too worried as we figured we could always use one of the smaller airlines to get us back to Wewak. It would take longer and would have more stops, but it could be done.

The next morning I saw the specialist. He checked things out and said he felt it would be another month before the baby arrived. Tim said, "So we'll come back in a month?" The specialist replied, "No, you can come back in a month. Your wife must stay here." There was a long pause before he continued, "If you can't find a place to stay, she can always stay at the hospital until the baby comes." The doctor told me to come back in a week.

Tim and I left his office, shocked by the developments. What were we going to do? The hotel we were in was lovely for a couple of nights, but it was too expensive for a long-term arrangement.

We started looking.

The Madang Country Women's Association advertised its guesthouse for 'women in distress'. That described our plight. Of course, when we got there, there were no vacant rooms.

We wandered around Madang that afternoon, finding the hotels too expensive, and the guest houses and hostels full. We eventually gave up looking and wandered over to a corner store to buy a newspaper, in which might be a solution.

Out of the blue came a voice, "What are you two doing here?" It was our old bank manager, from a previous place where we had lived. Tim gave him a quick rundown of our situation. When he had finished, this kind man suggested that we go to his house and meet his wife.

This bank manager had a lovely home, overlooking the sea. There was an extra bedroom and bathroom they weren't using. His wife was delighted she would have company. Tim had already discovered that a boat left the Madang Harbour on Friday morning, as he had to go back to work, so we arranged that I would be picked up from the hotel when Tim had gone. Things were looking up. Tim would return to Madang until I went into labour, probably at the end of May.

We returned to the hotel and talked about the next few weeks. I said, "It would be so much easier if the baby was born tonight." And, lo and behold, that's what happened.

I felt that labour had started later in the evening. At 10:00pm, the specialist suggested we come to the hospital. By 10:30, I was ushered to a room by a nurse whose sister was a student at our school. The specialist arrived, checked things and declared I was in labour and the safest avenue was a caesarian.

The doctor moved quickly. "Send the ambulance out to find the operating staff," he said to the nurse. She left and he told us that it would take a while before everyone was in place. "We don't often operate at night so we don't keep the staff here. They know they are on call but we have to find them. No one has a telephone. Usually, if people aren't at home, they might be at the movies or visiting friends. Don't worry. The ambulance will find them."

Just after midnight on May 2nd 1980, they

wheeled me outside to an adjacent building that housed the operating room. The last thing I remember is looking at the blackboard on the wall where they had written the total number of sponges they had. Next to that column was another, titled 'used'. It was blank.

Tim told me later that the baby was out within 5 minutes. She weighed 2.3 kg and, of course, was perfect. It took longer for me to leave the operating room so Tim had time to look at the nursery and then return to find me.

Once he knew both of us were okay, he returned to the hotel and explained to the night clerk what had happened and asked if he could make a phone call to my parents in Canada and his parents in England. As it turned out, the night clerk had also been a student of ours and he couldn't do enough. Tim was terrified of the phone bill, but the hotel clerk only charged him for 2 local calls.

My mother in Sault Ste Marie, Ontario, was thrilled because she thought she had a May Day grandchild. What she hadn't taken into account was the fact that although it was the afternoon of May 1st in Canada when Tim called, it was actually early in the morning of May 2nd in Papua New Guinea because of the International Date Line.

We had nothing with us for the baby to wear. We hadn't thought of a name. We didn't have a crib or a car seat or toys. It wasn't long before people started to arrive at the hospital with things for the baby.

Papua New Guineans use the word 'wantok' to describe a person who is from your family, your village, or your language group. It didn't matter that Tim and I were not Papua New Guinean. Relations of students we had taught, students from the teachers' college, and the bank manager and his wife all brought clothing to the hospital.

Naming her was more difficult. We had to have a name before we left the hospital. Tim and I each made lists separately and them compared them. There was not a lot of common ground. As teachers we were also aware of the problems created by children with non-traditional names. I was reading about Nicholas and Alexandra – the story of the last Tsar and Tsarina of Russia. We feminized Nicholas to Nichola, Kathleen was my mother's name, and Sarah was the name of one of my oldest friends.

By the weekend, the planes were flying again and we were able to fly back to Wewak. We borrowed a crib and Nichola settled in as though she had been there forever.

★★★

I went back to work at the beginning of July and a new routine began. At Passam, the electricity was provided by a generator that was started at 6 am and shut off at 10 pm. We would wake up at about 5.30 am. I would deal with the baby and Tim would take the car and pick up Winnie, the babysitter. I usually drove her back in the afternoon.

We had a Suzuki 4 wheel drive that was a box on wheels. It could easily be identified because it sounded like a lawn mower. It only had two bucket seats so if Nichola came with me in the car, I put her in a cardboard box on the floor on the passenger side. I am sure baby car seats were in use in North America in 1980 but we had no idea how to get one in Papua New Guinea. Everyone held their babies in the front of cars, in the back of trucks.

One Friday afternoon, we were later than normal getting back from school. Tim suggested that it might be better if he drove Winnie home while I got Nichola ready for bed and made supper. I felt that he had suggested the change so that he could have the relaxing drive while I hustled around, doing all the things that needed to be done. I won the argument, took the keys, and left for the village with the babysitter.

We had left the school and were on the main road when I heard the lub-lub-lub noises associated with a flat tire. I pulled over to the side of the road, cursing. The roads were made out of crushed coral and flat tires were a common occurrence. The jack was stored under the front seat or was supposed to be stored under. I couldn't find it.

Having made the point before I left the house that I was perfectly capable of taking the babysitter home, I didn't feel that I could go back and ask Tim where the jack was. I could handle this.

There was a mission station on the other side of the road and I was sure the priest would lend me a jack. I walked up the hill to talk to the priest. He was very obliging but only had the jack that came with his coffee truck. He thought it might be a bit big. I shrugged off his concerns and walked back to the car with the jack over my shoulder.

I placed the jack under the car on the side with the flat tire. I pulled the handle of the jack and nothing happened. So, I pulled again and immediately saw the side of the car rise and slowly begin to tip over. I hadn't stopped on a flat piece of road and realized when it was too late. I was powerless to stop the car going over on its side.

Disaster always attracts a crowd and within minutes village people, school children, and the priest had arrived to gawk at what I had done. However, they helped. One man climbed onto the side of the car and took off the flat. Another man got the spare and passed it up to him. It was attached and before I knew it, a group of men had righted the car. I thanked them, got in the car, and continued driving the babysitter home.

Although I told Tim about the flat tire, it was months before I told him how it was changed.

★★★

One morning, the alarm went off and I tried to get out of bed. The house was moving so much, it was difficult. I woke Tim up and mentioned 'earthquake.' He immediately said, "Grab the baby and go outside. If you don't get out in the first 30 seconds it doesn't matter anymore."

In those days in the tropics, we didn't wear pajamas. I said, "But I don't have any clothes on." To which he replied, "It doesn't matter. It's an emergency. No one will notice." I struggled into the baby's room and was on my way, naked, to the living room when I happened to glance back. There was Tim, wrapped in our orange bedspread, trying to lift a 4-drawer filing cabinet over his shoulder.

"What are you doing?" I shouted, eying the bedspread jealously.

"The passports are in here. We have to have the passports," he replied, breathing heavily.

"They're not in there, you know. They're on the desk. I took them out yesterday," I said and watched while he dropped the cabinet.

The 30 seconds had long since passed. The

house had stopped shaking. The only thing moving was the Coleman lamp that was attached to a nail in the centre beam of the living room. We looked at each other. "How come you got the bedspread?" I asked.

The couple that lived beside us had no children and both raced out of their house, naked, carrying their clothes, within the 30 seconds. Phil told us later that as both he and his wife tried to dress themselves, they were terrified that at any moment, the power would come on and so would the outside lights, illuminating them as they dressed.

In the house next to Phil, there was a new English recruit and his wife and 3 year old daughter. They didn't know what to do, so they all got under the bed. Another couple raced outside and then had a loud argument over who should go back in and get their 4 year old son who was still asleep.

★★★

Shortly after the earthquake, we were invited to return to Milne Bay to start a high school at

Losuia on the island of Kiriwina, which was one of the Trobriand Islands.

Although we had both been to Kiriwina when we'd lived in Milne Bay, I don't think either of us realized the challenges that lay before us. Our job was to build a high school so that children finishing elementary school would not have to leave home to go to the mainland for high school. Places in the high schools on the mainland were allocated by a quota system based on examination marks and location. There were never enough places for all the qualified students, so many students from the Trobs never made it to high school.

Nichola was 8 months old when we landed on the gravel airstrip at Losuia. Losuia had an aid post, a police station, a post office with a radio telephone, and a trade store. We were the only non-native people living in Losuia, although there was a Catholic mission and a small hotel further out of town, both run by Australians.

★★★

In the two years we lived on Losuia, we had

7 days of electricity, but never enough pressure to have water run through the pipes. All the water we used came from rain collected in large tanks beside the house.

Our first house was at the crossroads of the community and we were the new people in town. We didn't have any curtains to begin with so our house became a reality television show for the community. People would sit on the grass outside our house and watch our meal preparations as well as our child management skills.

When you live in the tropics, near the equator, sunrise and sunset are at about the same time every day. It doesn't change very much throughout the year. When you have no electricity, you have to make sure that all the jobs you need to do are done before it gets dark as you only have a flashlight or a kerosene lantern to see by.

We had only been in the house for a short few days when the unexpected happened. I fed Nichola, washed her, and put her to bed. It was just after 6 pm and it was almost dark. She refused to lie down and sleep. I shut the door to her room and came out to the living room, leaving her crying.

Tim said, "I think we should pick her up."

I replied, "No, then she'll think we will pick her up every time she cries. We don't want to spoil her. Let's just leave her."

So we did. We went out and sat on the porch of the house, watching the sunset. All of a sudden we heard the back door open. We went back inside and a woman rushed past us carrying Nichola. She said, "We don't let our babies cry here." As they disappeared down the back steps, Tim and I looked at each other. We were too stunned to move. "Where do you think she's taken her?' I asked Tim.

Tim said, "She can't have gone far. It is an island. I'll go next door and see what Alan suggests." Alan was the primary school inspector, his wife was one of the nurses at the aid station. Tim found the woman and Nichola at Alan's house. Nichola was happily playing in the dirt with the other children. The woman proceeded to lecture Tim on the evils of letting children cry. She let him take Nichola back but warned him that she would do it again if she heard Nichola crying.

So, we got coverings for the windows and were very careful to make sure Nichola didn't cry in the evenings. Eventually, we moved house and found ourselves further back from the road, but we continued to make sure she didn't cry herself to sleep. When Nichola eventually moved to a bed, one of us would always lie down beside her until she went to sleep, always wary that the crazy lady would hear her crying and come and get her again.

Over time, we settled into life at Losuia. During the week, Tim and I would go to work, dropping Nichola off at Rose and Ernest Goweli's house in the village. She was treated like their own daughter, fed the food of the village, taken to all the celebrations, and watched like a hawk. She was the only blond child on the island. Everyone wanted to touch her skin and feel her hair because it was so different than everyone else's.

As Nichola learned to walk and talk, she also learned to speak Kiriwinian. Everyone except Tim and I and an Australian nun, Sister Helen, spoke to her in Kiriwinian. She had very few toys because there was nowhere to buy them. She played with pots and pans, sticks and stones, and enjoyed the beaches on the weekends.

We had no running water and no electricity.

There was a bathtub, a shower, a toilet and a sink in the house. In years gone by, there must have been enough fuel to run the generator, which provided electricity for Losuia. If the electricity ran long enough, water could be pumped through the pipes and into the house. That never happened while we lived there.

In the early evening, I would put a saucepan full of water on the gas stove to heat. I would then pour it and some cold water in a red bowl on the porch. Nichola would have a bath and get ready for bed. Tim would read to her while I took Nichola's bath water and filled the bucket shower and had my own wash. I would catch the water in another bucket for Tim. He would put the water back in the shower bucket and have a shower while I put Nichola to bed. Tim would catch his water in a bucket and before we went to bed, he would flush the toilet with it.

The only fresh water we had came from the rain tank beside our house. The tank was 1000 gallons and had to last us from one rainfall to the next. It was never full and having enough fresh water was always a worry.

Because we had no electricity, the fridge that was in the house when we moved in was really a cupboard where we stored food. If we gave Nichola a bottle in her crib, it was an invitation to all the cockroaches and ants to come and join her. Rose, the woman who looked after Nichola, suggested that we put the legs of the crib in tin cans of water. The tin cans had to be big enough so that the insects couldn't reach the crib legs. We just had to remember to change the water often so mosquitoes wouldn't use it as a breeding area.

Eventually, the Education Department issued us with a kerosene fridge, which meant our food choices expanded. We had a lot of canned food shipped by boat from the mainland. We had tinned hot dogs, chicken, and ham as well as tinned vegetables. When we opened the tin of chicken, a whole chicken slid out, covered in a gelatin-like substance. It would sit on a plate and as the gelatin fell off, the wings and the legs would sort of spring into place. We had 2 gas burners on the top of the stove that worked. The oven never did. A previous tenant had tried to burn wood in the oven and had wrecked it.

We would buy fresh food from people who came to the house: sweet potatoes, yams, and tapioca. The students built gardens and we could buy greens and tomatoes from them. There was always fish, coconuts, papayas, bananas, and green oranges. Nichola never had fresh milk, it was all powdered, and she ate what we ate because there was no baby food. I mashed everything with a fork until she could chew.

One night, just after midnight, Nichola woke, crying. Tim got out of bed and went next door to Nichola's room and lay down on the bed with her. Both of them fell asleep. I awoke just after one, smelling beer in the bedroom. All I could think of was how strange it was for Tim to have a beer at this time of night. When I opened my eyes, I could see a strange man in the room. I didn't actually scream but I called, "Tim, there's somebody in our room!"

Normally, Tim would never have woken with me just calling out to him. Something made him jump out of the bed in Nichola's room and back into ours. Just as he came through the doorway, the man who had been standing there, looking at me, raised his arm and struck Tim with a small axe. Luckily, it was our axe and not very sharp. It glanced off Tim's head and landed in his shoulder.

Tim shouted at me, "Get the flashlight."

We always kept one by the side of the bed. It seemed to take me forever to find it. Meanwhile, the guy had dropped the axe and Tim had wrestled the man to the floor. Holding him by his ears and his hair, Tim banged his head on the floor several times before I managed to turn on the flashlight. As luck would have it, Tim looked up and the beam of light blinded him momentarily. He loosened his grip on the man, who then made a run for the door and left the house.

The police arrived shortly after the intruder left. Their office was about 250 metres from our house and someone must have reported the commotion. They made sure we were all right and said they would find the man who had broken into our house in the morning.

After they left, we started going down the hall and back to bed. Our flashlight was still on and we saw liquid on the floor. Tim figured it was blood. He said, "I know I bit the guy but I didn't realize just how hard."

It was then that I looked at his back. There was blood all over it from the axe attack.

I guess we could have gone to the first aid clinic but they had no electricity either and only limited first aid material. I figured I could handle it. I remembered watching Westerns, where they poured alcohol on bullet wounds so I did the same thing with the cut. I then got some Elastoplast bandage material we had and attached it as best I could, and then we went back to bed. Nichola never woke up.

The next day, the police arrived before we went to school. "We found him," they said, "in a village not far from here. He had Schweppes tonic water cans in his possession. You can't buy that kind here. Can you come and identify him?"

We went over to the police station. Four young men were there. Tim recognized the intruder immediately and started to go after him, something he'd never done before or since. He was restrained by the police.

"Why did you do it?" Tim asked, "Why?"

The man didn't answer at the time but later we found out why. He was the older brother of one of our students. He had not been accepted to high school when he finished Grade 6. Since we had started the high school, many Grade 6 students who previously would not have gone to high school were going. He was angry at the system and Tim and I represented the system so he took it out on us.

★★★

Saturday was mail day for the two years we lived on the Trobriand Islands. Tim had himself made honourary postmaster for Saturdays. He would get a ride out to the airport, get the mail bags off the plane, take them to the post office and sort the mail. The regular postmaster was quite happy to leave the mail in the bags until Monday morning and regular post office hours. We couldn't. We were mail dependent – it was our weekly link to the outside world.

Nichola always woke up with the sun, about 6 am. This particular Saturday I was tired and really wanted to finish a new book I had been reading.

I'd read all her books to her, we'd played all the games I could think of, and so I suggested to Tim that he take her out to the airport with him.

Tim took the hint and said, "Stay here, relax, finish your book, put your feet up. We'll have a great time." So Tim and Nichola went off in the school truck with Ernest.

I figured I would have two hours and had just snuggled into my favourite chair with a book when I heard someone coming up the stairs. It was Mispah, Rose's sister, who helped look after Nichola during the week. "I've just bought over some bananas for Nichola." I thanked Mispah and returned to my 'quiet' time.

All of a sudden, there were footsteps running up the stairs. "Quick, missus," said Mispah breathlessly, "there's a snake going into your house."

I went outside with a sinking feeling in the pit of my stomach. Sure enough, a large snake between two and three metres long had curled itself around the sewer pipe and was slowly making its way into the house through a gap between the pipe and the siding. My quiet time was gone.

I ran over to the police station to ask for help.

Immediately, the three policemen on duty ran to my house. A number of people joined the police, so there were about 20 people watching the bottom half of the snake trying to get through the hole. The top half had already made it.

The police officer in charge said, "We'll go into your house and see where the snake is." I was in no position to argue and soon 20 people were in my house, arguing about where the snake was because they couldn't see it.

The eventual consensus was that the snake was between the siding on the outside and the interior bathroom walls. There was nothing for it, they'd have to rip out the bathroom wall. I agreed because my worst nightmare would be a snake on the loose between the walls of my house. So, everyone left to go and get their tools.

I found myself sitting at the table wondering what I'd done to deserve this. There was a knock on the door. Mispah's brother, Peter, was there. He said, "Don't worry. I'll get the snake for you."

I followed him outside and as I watched, he grabbed the tail of the snake just before it disappeared into the bowels of my house, and yanked.

The whole snake fell out. He picked up a rock and killed it and left the carcass in our driveway. I thanked Peter and he disappeared.

Meanwhile, the 20 people including the police arrived back, armed with tools they felt were appropriate to rip the walls out of my house and also kill the snake. They were disappointed to find that the problem had been solved. The excitement was gone from their day.

I had just returned to my book when Tim arrived home with the mail and Nichola. "Did you have a nice quiet time?" he asked.

★★★

After Nichola learned how to walk and talk, all she knew was Losuia and life on the island. One day Tim went to pick her up from Rose's house and he found her with a machete in one hand and a coconut in the other. Mispah, Rose's sister was watching her as she tried to crack the coconut.

Tim shouted, "She's going to cut herself." Mispah said, "Why? She knows what she is doing," and Tim watched as Nichola managed to cut the coconut in half. Nichola had watched everyone crack a coconut and when she felt she could do it, she did. That was how children learned in the village.

At the beginning of our second year on Trobs, one of the British volunteers in Alotau contacted us. "We're going back to England," he said, "and we need somebody to take our cat. If you take our cat, we'll give you our car."

He went on to explain that although the car ran, it wouldn't go up any hills. Everyone in Alotau knew this and so no one would buy it. He also knew that there were no big hills where we lived and we could certainly use a vehicle. We agreed.

A friend in Alotau said he would give the car a tune up and put it on the next barge coming out to the island. The cat arrived by air, a lovely ginger tom who was completely independent and only needed us for food and an occasional stroke. The car arrived a few weeks after the cat. It was a Mazda 929 station wagon, rusting but running.

The students were just as excited as we were. Everyone wanted to go for a ride. There had been trucks on the island for years but not a car with a back seat, at least in living memory. We gave rides to everyone who wanted one and then we headed home.

That evening we decided we would go to the Kiriwina Lodge for supper. When Rose arrived, Tim and I left in our car for an evening out. Just before we got to the lodge, there was a strange noise.

"Stop. Tim," I said, "I think there is something wrong."

"There's no point in stopping here. We can't see anything. We might as well keep going to the lodge and someone there can look at it," Tim responded. He was right, of course. It was really dark, there were no street lights, and all we could see was what the car's headlights illuminated.

"Tim, the car feels wobbly," I replied, not knowing how else to describe the strange vibrations. Just after I said those words, the front tire on the passenger's side rolled away from the car, leaving us momentarily suspended on three wheels. We watched it roll down the road in front of us, lit up by the headlights.

Tim put his foot on the brake and as we

slowed down the car eventually tipped down to rest on the axle. The headlights showed the tire disappearing across the road, down a gully, up the other side and into some jungle. Tim passed me the flashlight.

"I'll get the tire," he said. "See if you can find the nuts." I bit back a sarcastic comment and dutifully got out of the lopsided car and proceeded to walk down the deserted road looking for wheel nuts. It was like looking for a needle in a haystack. Tim had the good job. A car tire was easy to find.

Eventually we decided that we weren't ever going to find the nuts. Tim had the brilliant idea of taking a nut off each of the other tires and reattaching the fourth tire. All the other nuts were very loose so he tightened those as well.

We never bothered getting any more nuts. Three seemed to work just as well as four and it made getting the tire on and off that much easier whenever we had a flat tire.

Later, we found out that our friend in Alotau had just finished putting on new brake pads when the call came to get the car down to the wharf right away because it was about to leave. He had thrown the tires on and attached the nuts but had forgotten to tighten them. When we picked up the car, we didn't think to check whether the nuts on the wheels needed tightening.

★★★

The car turned out to be remarkably useful. The District Officer in Charge (DOIC) of the Trobriand Islands discovered that the New Zealand High Commissioner and his wife were coming on an official visit to the island. He came to the school and asked if the car could be used to chauffeur then round the island. Tim agreed and then was asked to be the driver.

The couple arrived on the Saturday morning plane and were due to depart on the Monday afternoon. Everyone went out to the airstrip to greet them. The car had been polished and swept out. It was as clean as a car that age and vintage could be. Nichola and I sat in the front with Tim driving. When we arrived at the airstrip, everyone laughed and waved.

Just before the plane arrived, the DOIC went

to see Tim. "Your wife and child cannot ride with you in the car," he said. "It wouldn't be right. They can go back to Losuia in one of the trucks."

His word was law and Nichola and I were now going to be one of the cheering throngs. It was disappointing.

The plane arrived. The New Zealand High Commissioner and his wife were easy to spot as they were the only two Europeans on the plane. The DOIC greeted them officially and then took them over to the Mazda 929 and introduced them to Tim. Once their luggage arrived, Tim had to lift their suitcases over the back seat into the cargo area as the trunk of the car had refused to open for some time.

The New Zealand High Commissioner started to get into the front of the car. Tim explained that they were both expected to ride in the back. So he held the door open for them and they both graciously squeezed into the back seat. As they drove towards town, they, of course, asked Tim why he was driving. He explained, "Our car was the only car with a back seat and air conditioning." As all the windows of the car were open and it was very hot, the New Zealand's High Commissioner's wife asked about the air conditioning.

"If you lift the plywood your feet are resting on, " Tim replied, "You'll find the air conditioning."

★★★

We were still at Losuia when I became pregnant with our second child. The closest doctor was on the mainland. Because of the nature of Nichola's birth I was concerned, and he suggested that I should be close to a hospital for the last 6 weeks of my pregnancy. He and his wife invited me to stay with them in Alotau, about an hour's flight from Losuia.

Tim and I went through the various options. All of them involved Nichola coming with me and the more I thought about it, the more I thought I'd like to be with my family. Six weeks with friends is a long time, six weeks with family can also be a long time but family members tend to be more honest and accepting.

I wrote to my parents, asking them if Nichola

and I could stay while we waited for the baby. They very generously agreed. It would be a huge inconvenience for them but I think their minds worked differently from ours. They felt they wouldn't have to worry about what was happening halfway around the world.

I was a returning resident. Nichola was on my passport but she had been registered at the British Embassy in Papua New Guinea. There was no Canadian Embassy and as Tim was British, it seemed to make sense. She had a British birth certificate, not a Canadian one.

I knew we should have done something before we left to return to Canada but Losuia was so far from anything that we just didn't do it. Instead, I booked our tickets so that we would fly into Sault Ste Marie, Michigan. I figured that as my parents lived in Sault Ste Marie, Ontario, they would be able to help me with any immigration issues.

We left Papua New Guinea at the beginning of October 1982. It was about 6 weeks before my due date. Luckily, I didn't look very pregnant but I did have a note from the doctor in Alotau stating that it was safe for me to fly.

Up until our trip, Nichola had only ever worn flip flops. She didn't have any shoes. We traced her feet on a piece of paper and arranged for a couple who came on a tour of the Trobs from Australia to buy her a pair of shoes. They came just before we left and Nichola proudly wore them to meet her grandparents.

She was remarkably well-behaved for a two year old. Everything was new to her so it wasn't hard to keep her entertained. We flew on and off for two days without actually sleeping in a bed. By the time I met my parents, I was pretty tired.

Just as I planned, we had to clear customs and immigration at the US-Canadian border. I went inside with Nichola to fill in the forms.

The immigration officer looked at the paperwork and said, "Your daughter does not have the right papers to reside in Canada."

I think he was going to say more but I interrupted him. I picked Nichola up and sat her on his desk and said, "I am just too tired. Why don't you keep her and I will come back tomorrow after I have slept and straighten the whole thing out."

The poor immigration official quickly said,

"That really won't be necessary. I just wanted to let you know that you need to file her citizenship forms as soon as you can."

When we arrived at my parents' house, my mother toured her around the house and showed her where she was going to sleep. My mother showed her the bathroom.

The toilet was perhaps the best toy my mother could have provided. No one could have had more joy flushing and reflushing the toilet than Nichola did. We had to drag her out of the bathroom for supper.

My mother had cooked three steaks for that first supper, and cut a bit off each one for Nichola, thinking that cooking a whole steak for a two year old would be a waste. Nichola hoovered up the pieces and then spent the rest of the meal looking for more. I am not sure that we had ever had fresh meat on the Trobs.

Nichola adjusted quickly to life in Sault Ste Marie. She called my mother Bubu, a Kiriwinan word meaning 'elder person'. My mother loved being called Bubu, and went by that name with all 13 of her grandchildren. My mother had found a preschool to which I took Nichola every morning.

In the afternoons, Nichola would nap and I would write to Tim. We knew that it would take at least two weeks for a letter to arrive, and then a further two weeks for a reply. He wanted to know how Nichola was adjusting, how my parents were adjusting, and when the baby would arrive.

Before we left Losuia, the Catholic Mission said they would be happy to take any messages from Tim. They had a SKED service, a short wave radio service that provided a daily scheduled time when all the mission stations would report to the mainland. News from the mainland would be reported out to the stations. And requests from the stations would be made back. It was a lifeline for the mission stations on remote islands.

The plan was for my father to telephone the Catholic Mission in Alotau on the mainland and let them know that the baby had arrived. They would then relay the message to Father Cunningham at Guseweta, about 15 kilometres from Losuia. Father Cunningham would get on his motorbike and deliver the message to Tim.

I carefully copied out the number of the

Catholic Mission as well as the international calling information and pinned it above the telephone at my parents' house.

Finally, the baby arrived on December 1st and the message relay began. My father called Alotau and the call was answered by Sister Helen, a nun from the Trobriand Islands who happened to be in Alotau. She was thrilled to be the one to pass on the message to Father Cunningham that afternoon. Father Cunningham got on his motorbike and rode as fast as he could on his Honda 70 to tell Tim.

Tim arrived in Sault Ste Marie when the baby was about three weeks old. For the first time, Nichola was old enough to understand Christmas and was the only child on which my four sisters and parents could dote. They got her so excited on Christmas Eve that she didn't go to bed until several hours after her normal bedtime.

In the morning, everyone crowded around this 2 year old child watching as she unwrapped all the educational toys my family had purchased. However, the mother of a friend of mine gave Nichola a princess doll and when Nichola unwrapped that, she could hardly breathe. Mrs Currie seemed to be the only person who understood what she really wanted for Christmas.

We returned to Papua New Guinea for one more year, this time in the Highlands. Nichola earned small amounts of money picking coffee beans with her babysitter. She learned to speak Tok Pigin and at one point was able to translate.

My sister Fiona had arrived for a visit. Tim and I went to school, leaving Nichola with the babysitter and Fiona. The babysitter put Victoria in a bilum (a string bag) and took Nichola's hand. Fiona asked, "Where are you going?" to the babysitter. She didn't speak any English. Nichola translated the question and waited for the response. "We're going to her house," said Nichola and left. My sister had no idea where they were going or what they were going to do but Nichola had every confidence that it was going to work out.

Even though Nichola was born in Papua New Guinea, and we enjoyed our work and our lifestyle there, we recognized that both our children would never be Papua New Guineans.

The urge to be back amongst our own

families was strong. We eventually decided on Canada: Tim felt that as Canada was good enough for Karsh and Leonard Cohen, it was good enough for him, too.

Once he received his landed immigrant status, we arranged our trip back to Canada, stopping for Christmas in Sydney, Australia for one last warm Christmas.

Canada

1984 - 1998

At the end of January 1984, we returned to Canada, planning to stay in Sault Ste Marie with my parents again while Tim and I figured out what we were going to do. We enrolled Nichola in her old preschool, which had moved into new premises at Etienne Brule Public School.

By the summer, we had teaching jobs at Black Lake, Saskatchewan, a Dene community about 60 kms south of the Northwest Territories. It was a fly-in community with no roads connecting it to the rest of Canada. Tim drove a U-Haul to Saskatoon and the girls and I flew and met him there.

Indian Affairs had chartered a plane to take teachers and their families to the small town of Stony Rapids. From there, one group went in smaller floatplanes to Fond du Lac, and the rest of us went to Black Lake in a variety of vehicles.

The girls and I sat in the front of a truck while Tim and the rest of the staff got to ride in the back of the closed-sided vehicle. There were no windows and for 16 long kilometres, they had no idea where they were.

Our time in Papua New Guinea had served us well and we came prepared with food, bedding and cooking utensils in our luggage. By the time we arrived in Black Lake, the store was closed and we ended up feeding the rest of the staff who weren't so prepared.

It didn't take long to settle in to our new life. Nichola was old enough to go to the afternoon junior kindergarten. Victoria stayed with the babysitter. It was hard to imagine a place more different than Papua New Guinea, but we liked the North and its people.

School ended for the Christmas holidays and we decided that we would stay in Black Lake. Tim and I didn't want the girls to get over-excited about Christmas. We didn't have a television and Nichola couldn't read – she was only 4. The Hudson Bay store had a few Christmas decorations but the girls didn't come with me when I went shopping.

Nichola knew about Christmas but had no idea when Christmas Day was. We had ordered Christmas presents from Sears and our families had sent gifts but they all arrived by mail and were delivered to the school. We left them there.

On Christmas Eve, we put the girls to bed. Tim picked up the gifts and brought them home. I began wrapping as he went out on the skidoo and cut down a tree by the light of the snowmobile. Christmas was ready by 11 pm. We filled the girls' stockings and laid them on their beds.

The girls woke up at their normal time and came into our room. "Guess what?" I said. "Today is Christmas!"

We had a lovely day. No one was tired or cranky. Tim and I were the only ones that noticed that it was minus 50 degrees Celsius. Exactly one year before, we had spent Christmas Day in Sydney, Australia on the beach.

The cold was fierce at Black Lake. We adjusted, sort of. In February, Tim as principal, sent staff home early at lunchtime. The water was going to be shut off for several days and we were told to collect as much as we could for cooking and cleaning. The alternative would be getting water from the lake. I went home and filled the bathtub first, thinking we could use the water for washing the girls and flushing the toilet. Once it was filled, Nichola asked, "Can Victoria and I play in the water?" I agreed they could.

I had forgotten that we had a 3 month old St Bernard puppy called Winston. Nichola, of course, encouraged the dog to jump into the bathtub with them. I heard the splashing and found the three of them having a great time but making a watery mess on the floor.

I took the dog and dragged him to basement and shut the door behind him, figuring he could dry off there. He began to whine and scratch and bark. I ignored it and began making lunch. Nichola heard the noise and couldn't stand to hear the dog crying so she opened the basement door and the dog raced back to the bathroom and jumped back into the tub. I grabbed Winston again but this time I put him out the front door. I then cleaned up the water, got the girls out of the tub and dressed and then got lunch on the table.

Tim arrived home and asked, "What's that lump of ice on the front porch?" I realized that it was the dog. Because it was so cold, he had pretty well frozen to one spot. We managed to free him from the ice and brought him inside and warmed him up. He recovered, but never went near the bathtub again.

It had been minus 40 degrees Celsius for weeks on end and we had all gotten used to it. It suddenly warmed up one day to about zero and as Tim and I walked home for lunch, we found Nichola and Victoria in bathing suits on the steps leading up to the house. They thought spring had arrived.

★★★

Because Black Lake was a fly-in community, the fresh food arrived once a week on the same plane as the mail. Whenever anyone went south, they took with them lists of shopping.

For a few weeks, the newly appointed director of education lived with us as his house was not ready. He had been down south for meetings and on his return, he decided to make us dinner with special ingredients he had brought back from Prince Albert.

Bill took over our kitchen on a Saturday and told us to go for a walk and come back at supper-time. We did as he asked and on our return could smell the most wonderful aromas. We sat at the table and Bill served us spaghetti alfredo which we had never had before. It was delicious and Bill had spent all afternoon making it. Nichola finished her pasta quickly, and turned to Bill and asked, "Can I have more Kraft dinner, please?"

★★★

Nichola began her formal education at Black Lake where the language of the playground in those days was Dene. There was no television in our first year and we relied on getting books from mail order places in England and Canada. Tim began reading *The Hobbit* to Nichola, a few pages a night. I was never allowed to read it to her because I couldn't do the voices properly.

Nichola began afternoon kindergarten in

September 1984. Within a few weeks, she was completely at home. Eventually, the basement became the girls' playground, especially when it got cold. All Nichola had to do was open the door and go outside to be immediately surrounded by children who wanted to play with her.

There was sand everywhere in the community and play was pretty rough and tumble. The girls took countless utensils outside to dig in the sand which they always lost. From the three years we were there, I am convinced there is a place setting for 6 people that anthropologists will find in years to come.

It's funny the things you worry about as a parent. In Black Lake, I worried about fire. In those days, if a house caught on fire, it just burned to the ground as there was no fire department. The first house I saw burn to the ground was because of children playing with matches.

When another house caught on fire for the same reason, I went home and took Nichola and Victoria to the fire. Within 15 minutes there was nothing left. All you could see was a metal bed frame, and the remains of a fridge and a stove. I remember telling them that this is what happens when you play with matches. Nichola told me much later that she was 18 before she struck her first match.

Over time, Nichola learned Dene, and participated in the life of the community. She lined up to get money on Treaty Day from Indians Affairs. She was rejected but that didn't stop her participating.

★★★

Black Lake was also a Catholic community and when a nun arrived in the community to take the Grade Ones for First Communion classes, Nichola went with them. I walked by her Grade 2 classroom one day and saw her standing with the other students saying, "I am a Chipewyan Indian." She ate dried meat, both caribou and moose, made by the women of the community, and liked it best with Tenderflake lard and bannock.

When we left Black Lake in June 1987, Nichola had skills that a 7 year old in an urban setting might not have. She could speak and understand the Dene language. She actually won a prize at school for being the 'most improved Dene speaker'. She knew the difference between a ptarmigan and a spruce grouse. She could bait a fish hook and clean a fish. She had flown to the tundra to watch the great caribou migration.

She didn't know any television shows but could do 'Layer Cake' on the computer. She could read completely independently, and amuse herself and her sister for hours building forts, playing school, and on one memorable occasion, hairdresser.

However, she could not ride a bicycle, jump rope, or know any tv shows. She had not been a Spark or a Brownie, nor taken swimming or piano lessons.

We arrived in Shields Townsite, near Dundurn, Saskatchewan, in June 1987. Tim was returning to the University of Saskatchewan in Saskatoon for a year to complete his B.Ed.

Shields was close to Blackstrap Mountain, 'the pimple on the prairie' built in the early 1970s for the Canada Winter Games. It was the only high ground: the rest was prairies, a great contrast to the boreal forest of northern Saskatchewan.

In a way, the two years in Dundurn introduced the girls to mainstream Canada. They took swimming lessons, learned how to skip, and after much help mastered the art of riding a two wheeler. They both took figure skating lessons—although as much as they wanted to skate for Canada, neither of them was very good.

The girls would catch the bus at about 7.45 am in the morning and return home around 4:00 pm. I would have a snack ready because I had learned that the girls were much happier having eaten something. We'd settle in to watch "Three's Company" and "Silver Spoons" on TV. At 5 pm, I turned off the TV and began making supper. The girls could use that time however they wished.

Tim would arrive home between 5 pm and 6 pm and ask if the girls had done their homework. I usually said I had no idea. Tim felt that I should be more involved than I was. He said several times, "The minute the girls get off the bus, they should do their homework. Then, they can play, watch TV, do whatever they want."

I replied, "My mother never made us do homework, she just expected us to do it. She said if the school ever called her and said we hadn't done our homework, she would get involved. I don't remember that ever happening. That," I said to Tim, "is what I want the girls to learn. It is not my responsibility to make them do their homework. It's theirs. I don't want it to be mine. I don't want to spend the next 20 years supervising homework, do you?"

So we agreed to use my method until it was shown not to work. There were a couple of incidents where Nichola had to set the alarm to get up early to finish something but no one ever phoned to say the girls had not done their homework. We would help if asked, but otherwise, let them do it on their own. My method worked all the way through elementary and high school.

★★★

By March of 1989 I could no longer hide the fact that I was pregnant from Nichola and Victoria. Neither Tim nor I were very good about sharing the facts of life so we were extremely uncomfortable sharing the news. Victoria at 6 ½ had heard on the playground about someone losing a baby. We reassured her that our baby was fine. All Nichola could say over and over again was, "I don't believe it, I just don't believe it." She did come round in time, though neither girl was very impressed with the makeshift babysitters that spring.

Tim accepted a position as principal of two schools in Pangnirtung on Baffin Island in April and we had to prepare our sealift order. The school board advanced money so that new teachers could get dry goods and frozen meats and vegetables for the year because of the high prices in the shops in Pang. I can remember a stalk of celery costing $9 and a 4 litre pail of ice cream being $28.

The lists of food came to us in French and we did our best but ended up with a few things we never used, including some tinned hot dogs—a crate of twelve boxes of twelve tins of hot dogs! I am not sure what we thought we were buying. We also had to include a crib and baby food with our order.

Kate was born on July 18th in Saskatoon and Tim was left with the two girls to pack the house by the beginning of August when we were flying east. One box arrived labeled 'Top of fridge' and I think in a desperate move to finish. Tim just ran his arm across the top of the fridge and everything that was there fell into a box.

By the time we moved to Pang in the summer of 1989, both girls were avid readers. Tim had completed his MEd at the University of Saskatchewan and accepted the job as principal for both Attagoyuk Ilisavik High School (Grades 6 -12) and Alookie School (Grades K – 5).

It was not one of our better moves. All the activities that Nichola and Victoria had enjoyed in Dundurn were not available in Pang. There were no trees, lots of ice, not much snow, and cold and dark between November and February.

We thought that the girls would have no trouble adjusting because of the other places they had lived. The girls worked hard at trying to make friends, inviting classmates over to the house, but adults were wary of newcomers, and their children picked up the feeling. Nichola asked us one day, "Why can't I make friends here?" It was difficult to explain to a 10 year old.

On a glorious spring day, Tim and Nichola

went for a dog sled ride with a friend from Pangnirtung. The ice was still in the fjord, although cracks were appearing. Tim was excited to take some action shots that would make him the envy of photographers everywhere.

Both Nichola and Tim travelled in the *komatiq*, the sled pulled by the dogs. The driver stood on the back of the sled, alternating running and riding. The dogs ran in a fan formation while they were on the ice. In Black Lake, when the dogs were on land, they ran in pairs, or single file through the woods.

About 2 hours from the community, they stopped for a break. There was a crack in the ice about a foot wide and Tim thought if he jumped across the crack and lay on the ice, he could get a great photograph of the dogs pulling the sled across the ice. He jumped across the crack – but the ice gave way and he went into the Arctic Ocean.

He was wearing Sorel boots, a parka, and snow pants and they immediately filled with water. Quick as a flash, the driver jumped off the sled and reached Tim just before he disappeared under the ice.

To this day, we have no idea how he managed to get Tim out of the water and onto the ice. All Nichola could do was watch. Tim ended up taking off all his outer wet clothes and Nichola snuggled in beside him in the sled, under a blanket, trying to prevent him from getting hypothermia.

As soon as they arrived back at the house, Tim got in the bathtub, gradually warming up the temperature of the water as he thawed out. It was a pivotal moment in Nichola's life. I don't think she ever wanted to feel that helpless again.

***

My father once told me that sometimes in life you make a mistake. The thing to do is to admit the mistake and move on. So Tim and I admitted that the move to Pangnirtung was a mistake and at the end of the school year, we packed up and took the three girls, and Winston, the aging St Bernard dog, to La Ronge, Saskatchewan.

La Ronge was half way between Black Lake and Dundurn, nearly at the end of the road. I'd made Tim promise that anywhere we moved to after Pangnirtung had to have running water, electricity, and a road going somewhere.

Tim and I bought our first house in La Ronge and we were finally able to get everything out of storage and out of my parents' attic. Nichola started Grade 5 at Pre-Cam School and finished Grade 7 at Churchill High School by the time we left three years later.

I had taken the girls out cross country skiing when we lived in Dundurn but although we had taken the skis with us to Pang, the ice made any cross country skiing challenging. La Ronge had fabulous trails at a park called Nut Point, which we walked for three seasons and skied in the winter. Nichola took to it like a duck to water and in her last year in La Ronge began racing competitively.

La Ronge had the first library the girls could access independently and quickly learned how the system worked and the joys of interlibrary loans.

Tim had introduced them to the fantasy world of Tolkien's *The Hobbit* and later, *Lord of the Rings* and they explored other fantasy writers. When a new David Eddings arrived in their name, Nichola would volunteer to do the dishes so Victoria could finish the book quickly and lend it to Nichola. Victoria read faster but Nichola liked having the book longer so she could read it over again immediately. Both girls felt they had the best of the deal.

★★★

There was a dental hygienist at the girls' school and at some point during their first year Nichola talked to her about the gap between her two front teeth. The dental hygienist called us, explaining that she had referred her to an orthodontist.

His office was in Prince Albert, a three hour trip each way. The orthodontist felt he could close the gap, and thus began our monthly trips to Prince Albert (PA), sometimes travelling six hours for a 5 minute appointment.

It was during one of those trips that Nichola and I decided to surprise everyone by getting a puppy at the Humane Society in PA. It wasn't just the puppy, we had to buy all the things a puppy needs. That was an expensive trip.

We arrived back home and I went in first to tell Tim and the girls that Nichola had a surprise for them. Tim said, "No, wait. I have a surprise as well."

Victoria came round the corner carrying a puppy called Petra that Tim had been given at work. Nichola entered the house carrying Charlie, the pound puppy.

It seemed to take a long time to train the puppies and there were always messes to clean up. One of the dogs actually carried in frozen poo to nibble on during the day, fondly remembered as the poopscicle.

★★★

The girls were also able to join Girl Guides again and I was able to help as a leader. The provincial Girl Guide organization sent a trainer to La Ronge to help with program details. Her mother-in-law had been the Queen's Guider, and she talked about the establishment of traditions within families.

Every Christmas she and her husband and

three girls would make a picnic and head into the woods, decorate a tree for the birds, have a winter picnic and cut down a Christmas tree and bring it home.

I thought this sounded like a great tradition that we could begin, especially in La Ronge where everyone just went off in the bush to get their tree. I mentioned it to Tim and he reluctantly agreed.

In previous years, Tim had taken the older two girls and the tree had always fit in the back of the Izuzu Trooper when part of the back seat was laid flat. With Kate and I now coming, he wasn't sure how everyone would fit with the tree.

I was one step ahead of him. I knew of 30 m of extension cord in the garage from the electric lawn mower that I ran over in the summer. I suggested that we could use it to tie the tree onto the roof of the car.

The morning of the Christmas tree/picnic/bird feeding was freezing. It was minus 40 C without the wind chill. Tim wisely suggested that all we could do was get the tree. The picnic and feeding the birds was not going to happen.

So, we all piled into the car and drove about

5 km out of town. We stopped and all got out. The trees were pretty well picked over so we all got back in the car and drove about 20 km up the highway and went on a side road for about a kilometre till we could go no further. We all got out. Tim led the way, carrying the axe over his should. Nichola was behind him, then Victoria, and then Kate and I.

Within 5 minutes Kate was crying because she was so cold. I got the keys from Tim and took her back to the car to warm up. Three minutes later, Victoria arrived, crying as well. "I picked a tree and Dad said it was no good," she sobbed.

Five minutes later, Nichola arrived, crying with tears of frustration. "Dad just won't listen. He just wants to pick what he wants." So now there were three sobbing children on the back seat.

Tim arrived, dragging a tree and carrying the axe. He was furious that the girls had deserted him. He threw the tree on the roof. "Open the windows," he demanded. We all opened them. He started to thread the yellow extension cord around the tree and through the windows.

"Pull it tight," he instructed, and we all pulled down on the cord. "Now tie a knot," he said. So,

I tied a knot. Then, he tried to open the driver's door, and it wouldn't open. We had to loosen the cord so the doors would open and Tim could get in the driver's seat. We drove to the highway and started the drive back to the house.

"Tim," I said, "The tree is slipping." "No, it isn't," he growled.

"The top of the tree is touching the highway," I said.

He pulled the car over to the side and said, "You drive!" So I crawled into the driver's seat.

Meanwhile, Tim climbed onto the hood of the car and pulled the tree back up by the trunk. He then got back in the passenger's side and told everyone to pull on the yellow cord as hard as they could. He tied a huge knot and pulled on the cord as we drove back to town. We pulled into the driveway and tried to undo the cord so we could get get out of the car.

Unfortunately, driving for half an hour in minus 40 degree temperatures meant that the extension cord was completely frozen. We all had to climb out the windows. Tim ended up borrowing bolt cutters from our neighbours to cut the cord.

To top it all off, the tree was too tall for the living room, and Tim had to chop the top off so we ended up with a squat Christmas tree. People came in, looked at the trunk, and went out to see whether the top was coming through the roof.

By the time the next Christmas rolled around, we were living in Edmonton, and we just picked a tree up at the mall. It was so much easier.

★★★

Nichola was 13 when we moved to Edmonton and enrolled in Grade 8 at Vernon Barford Junior High School. I don't think anyone could have had a better time. I often worried about all the moves we made and wondered how it would affect the girls. Nichola seemed to thrive on it. Whatever mistakes she'd made in the previous place, she made sure she didn't do them again. For her, it was like having another chance.

Nichola joined the cross country ski team and every week we drove her to practice in a big park down by the river. We'd drive there along the Whitemud highway, and it was always dark and cold. The smoke from the exhaust pipes of the cars was like a mist, and the car windows were always steamed up a bit, so whoever was driving really had to focus.

One evening, Nichola said, "Oh, it's -7 degrees. I'll need the BLUE wax."

Sure enough, when we got to the park, the coach said, "Blue wax tonight, guys."

Driving home later, Tim asked her, "How did you know that?"

Nichola explained. "We learned it in science. The angle of the car exhaust smoke changes depending on temperature."

"Oh," said Tim, "OK."

Tim told me later how clever it was to make the science curriculum so adaptable to the real world instead of being vague and not very relevant.

This continued for a few weeks. Nichola would say the temperature and predict the wax colour and she was always right. Both Tim and I were impressed. Then one day, Victoria came along for the ride. She said, "Wow, it's really cold, -21."

Tim asked her, "How do you know that?"

"It's on the thermometer, look!" she said,

pointing to this building on the side of the road. There was a temperature thermometer and a clock blinking away on the top of it, but Tim had never seen it because he had always focused on the road and the cars around him and their exhausts.

Nichola laughed. It gave her enormous joy to catch her father.

Nichola also earned the nickname Carebear while racing with the cross country ski team. One of her team members had an asthma attack and Nichola stopped her race and skied back with him, making sure he arrived safely.

Nichola delivered flyers in a neighbourhood close to ours. The flyers would be dropped off at our house and she would load them in a shopping cart and disappear for several hours. It wasn't until Tim and I had to do it once that we realized that it only took an hour.

Nichola had a 'friend' who 'helped'. Matt was a nice fellow who often got into trouble. Nichola would always tell us his latest antics around the dinner table. One I remember specifically was the winter day when he was asked to clean the ice off his mother's Miata convertible. He thought the weedwhacker would be much faster than the ice scraper. His mother had to get the whole car re-painted.

They were great friends, and although we were no longer living in Edmonton when he graduated, we got Nichola a plane ticket, and she flew out to be Matt's date.

Nichola began rowing on the river in the spring of 1995. Her braces had come off and she began separating boys into two categories—friends and dates. She met and began dating a real romantic at the rowing club. He would show up carrying one red rose. He was visiting one day, and the doorbell rang. He said, "Oh. My parents are picking me up." I opened the door and there was an older woman holding hands with a much younger man. It turned out that his father was married to his grandmother. We're still trying to work that one out.

In a way, Tim and I were glad Nichola spent that summer babysitting for my sister, Alison, in Arnprior, Ontario. We thought that the separation would be good for both of them. Of course, Nichola, found another 'friend' there.

Alison felt sorry for Nichola at 15, being stuck for the summer with her three young children. She introduced Nichola to the lifeguard at the local beach. Nichola dragged the kids to the beach every day that summer, rain or shine.

After the initial introduction, Alison and Jeff (my sister's husband) couldn't get rid of him. He would show up around 10 pm with videos. Their date was on an old couch in the basement of Alison and Jeff's house. At one point, Alison tried to talk to her about having a boyfriend.

Nichola said to her, "Do you think I am going to get pregnant?" Naturally, that is exactly what Alison thought, but she couldn't say that. She had not had a teenager so had no idea what to say.

At one point, Nichola asked if she could go to his island for the weekend. Details were pretty fuzzy when Alison asked who else was going to be there. Nichola said, "Why? Don't you trust me?"

Jeff then took over and said, "Call your father and tell him you are going to this island with your boyfriend by yourself. If he says it's okay, then you can go." Tim never got that call.

The day before Nichola returned to Edmonton, she was showing off swimming, probably to the lifeguard, and hit her front tooth against a rock in the water. Half her front tooth broke away and was lost in the Ottawa River.

Tim and I were quite upset as her braces had only come off the spring before she left Edmonton. Luckily, we found an excellent dentist in Edmonton who managed to restore the tooth. I don't think anyone ever knew. However, the gap came back.

Nichola returned just in time to help pack the U-Haul .Tim had been appointed to the Faculty of Education at Saint Francis Xavier University (StFX) in Antigonish, Nova Scotia.

I drove the Izuzu Trooper loaded with bikes on the roof, a Thule carrier for the skis and camping equipment, and all our luggage for an 8 day drive across Canada. Kate and Nichola travelled with me.Victoria played the flute across the country and navigated for the rest of us from the front of the U-Haul truck with Tim.

We stopped to visit my sister Elizabeth in Winnipeg. Tim drove the U-Haul into her driveway and then couldn't get it out. A kind neighbor who drove trucks for a living got it out for us.

After that, we were careful always to park facing forwards as reversing was not easy. We also spent the night in Arnprior so Nichola was able to have one last romantic evening with the lifeguard. We arrived in Antigonish Labour Day weekend and started school and work the very next day.

Tim had rented a house about 30 minutes from town, which meant all three girls had to take the bus. The first day Tim and I registered Kate at H.M. MacDonald Elementary School in Maryvale, and Victoria at St Andrew's Junior High School in Antigonish. Nichola was going into Grade 10 and we had made an appointment with the guidance office at Dr. J.H. Gillis Regional High School, so Nichola could select courses.

There were core courses that she had to take but she could choose several electives. One she selected was Geography. The guidance counselor tried to persuade her to take something else. "It's not really an academic course," he said. "Anybody can take it, regardless of ability." Nichola was not deterred. "I think it is a good fit for me," she said. "I've travelled a lot. I know quite a bit already." So, she enrolled in Grade 10 Geography. On the positive side, she made a best friend.

She and her new friend took the same bus so ended up working on a geography project together. I drove to pick Nichola up at her friend's house. They had been assigned glaciers and for some reason thought that Styrofoam and cotton wool and a glue gun would explain its workings. I couldn't believe they were going to hand it in to be marked.

When the first marks were distributed, Nichola had failed Geography. It had never happened before. Tim had trained in geography at Teachers' College in England. We had travelled, had always talked to the girls about geographical features.

Tim and I went to Parent-Teacher interviews, determined to find out what had gone wrong. The line up for the geography teacher was the longest. Almost every student had failed and all the other parents were just as upset as we were. I had visited all of Nichola's other teachers before Tim got to the front of the line. It turned out that few students passed the first test, and fewer passed the project.

Nichola had complained that the course wasn't what she expected, but then, we explained, not everything is. The teacher was not going to change his expectations. Nichola and the other students would have to change theirs.

She was studying for the end of year geography exam and she came to me and said, "I know this is going to be on the exam." I said, "Do you know it?" Nichola said, "No, I don't see why I need to memorize it." I said, "If you know it is on the exam, and don't memorize it, who wins?" Ultimately, Nichola did well in geography, but it took her quite a while to conform to what the teacher wanted rather than what she felt she should be learning.

Nichola also had to take gym and part of that meant taking gymnastics. The girls were divided into groups of 4 and had to prepare a gymnastic routine for the rest of the class to enjoy and assess. The students had several gym periods to get their routine ready. The groups all around Nichola prepared handstands and summersaults and floor routines.

Nichola's group was not very athletic nor very motivated but Nichola got everyone running on the spot and then log rolling. When we met the gym teacher later at Parent-Teacher interviews, she was incredibly complimentary about Nichola's ability to pull a group together and do something.

★★★

One night at dinner, Nichola told us that she had gotten into trouble at school that day. She thought that the principal might call.

It was cow eye dissection day in Biology. Nichola was with her group of four or five students. The cow eye was in the centre of the table. Someone at the table dared another student to eat it. He refused. Then everyone at the table offered five dollars each. The student reached over, put it in his mouth and swallowed it.

The biology teacher arrived to see how the dissection was going and quickly discovered what had happened to the eye. The student who'd swallowed it happened to be the principal's son. He was sent to the office and then to the hospital to be checked. Meanwhile the table group was asked to go to the office.

The principal gave them a stern lecture and

then said he was going to suspend the ringleader. Nichola told him, "If you are going to suspend him, you are going to have to suspend all of us."

Victoria, who was at high school by this time, said the story had taken all of one period to make the rounds of the school. The boy who had eaten the eye had his stomach pumped and was none the worse for wear, but they stopped dissecting eyes after that. He kept the twenty dollars.

★★★

Soon after arriving in Nova Scotia, Nichola connected with the Nova Scotia Cross Country Ski Team. She was warmly welcomed into their circle. Coaches helped her develop an individualized training program as she was the only racer in Antigonish.

The first year was challenging because there was not a lot of snow where we were living. I can remember Nichola dragging snow on a toboggan to make a ski track of about 30 metres behind our house. She would zip backwards and forwards on the track after school.

Once we moved to our new house in Maryvale, Nichola bought a pair of roller skis and trained on the paved roads in the area. I would often get up early in the morning to drive Nichola to the local ski hill where there was snow. I would sit in the car and watch Nichola skate ski up the hill and ski back down several times before she went to school. She would change in the car and be ready for school when I dropped her off.

I drove three of the team members to a race at Val Cartier just outside of Quebec City. One of the girls arrived from Cape Breton on the bus and overnighted with us. We left around 6 am and stopped in the Wentworth Valley to pick up another girl. I then drove the next 11 hours to Quebec City.

It was like a slumber party in the car, with the girls paying absolutely no attention to me. Bits of conversation stuck with me. "What do you mean you don't have a TV? Tell your parents to get one so you'll have something to talk about." That conversation went on for quite a long time as both Nichola and another girl did not have a TV and the third girl just didn't understand what people did when there was no TV. There was talk of books, of hobbies, of school, of skiing. In the 12 hours, I don't remember any silence.

Once I crossed the bridge over the St Lawrence River and arrived in Quebec City, I asked the girls to help me by reading the map. GPS and cell phone apps had not yet been invented. They paid absolutely no attention to me. Eventually, I had to pull over and demand that they read the map.

We made our way to the military base at Val Cartier where we were all staying. The first race was the next day. I can't remember how the girls did but the race the following day was cancelled because it was too cold. We turned around and drove all the way back.

Nobody seemed to mind that there had only been one race, and the slumber party continued.

Our house was almost half way between Halifax where the ski coach lived and the Cape Breton Highlands where the ski trails were. There was a constant flow of athletes and parents either dropping Nichola off or picking her up.

Nichola returned one day from a weekend

racing in The Cape Breton Highlands. There were three racers in the back seat of a small car, the coach and another adult were in the front seat. They were climbing up one of the mountains and the snow was blowing all around them, making the drive extremely difficult.

Suddenly, the driver stopped and said, "I can't see anything but I know there is something on the road."

When the wind died down for a couple of minutes, they could see the legs of a moose in front of the car. The body was level with the roof.

They were incredibly lucky that day. A car is no match for a moose.

★★★

In the fall of 1997, Nichola was in Grade 12. "If anyone asks me one more time what I am going to do, I'll scream," she would say. Her marks were good and as universities and colleges visited her high school, she went to many presentations. I wanted her to go to Trent University where I had gone and she applied there.

We had talked about the Royal Military College because I had once gone to a dance there and mentioned that the tuition was free. When the military did a presentation at the school, Nichola went. She became enamored with the possibilities.

"Free education and a job for five years after graduation," said Nichola one night after dinner. I reminisced nostalgically about my evening there at the Christmas ball. All the men were wearing red serge and their dates were all in ball gowns. It was in a wood paneled room that was decorated for Christmas.

Nichola began the application process. Tim and I decided that the 9 page application was the first challenge. Because Nichola had not been born in Canada, we had to find all the paperwork about her birth, her arrival in Canada, and the date she became a Canadian citizen. This meant digging around in boxes that had not been opened for some time. Nichola persevered with us, and ultimately, the application went off.

In January 1998, Nichola and another student from the Regional High School were invited to formal interviews in Sydney, Cape Breton. They spent a day doing medical, physical, and psychological testing. If you passed the first one you went to, you were sent on to the next one. If you didn't pass, you were shown the outside door.

They both passed and were told that they wouldn't know if they had been accepted until May and to make sure they applied to other post secondary institutions in case they were not accepted to the Royal Military College (RMC) in Kingston, Ontario.

In May, Nichola heard she had been accepted and things moved quickly after that. In early June, Nichola along with other students from Nova Scotia who had been accepted into the Regular Officers' Training Program (ROTP), were invited to a swearing-in ceremony at the Lieutenant-Governor's house in Halifax on Friday June 19th 1998. Some of the students would go to regular universities and do military training in the summer. Others would go to RMC.

In later years, Nichola talked about the military being the great leveler. I think the seeds were sown that day. Everyone there that day had a different story to tell.

Some felt the military was the only way they could get an education because they couldn't afford to attend a regular university. Some joined for adventure, others to be able to fly jet planes or drive big trucks. Their parents were tradespeople, doctors, lawyers, teachers, waitresses, car salesmen, and retired military service people. But that day, it didn't matter because they all began their journey in the same way, scared about what was to come.

The day after Nichola's graduation, Tim and I got up at 3:30 am to drive her to Sydney, Cape Breton where she was to catch a plane to Montreal and begin her Basic Officers Training Course (BOTC) at the Saint-Jean Garrison in St. Jean-sur-Richelieu.

As we waved her off, neither she nor Tim and I had any idea what she was heading into.

The Military

1998 - 2006

We next heard from Nichola a week or two later. When Nichola was born in Papua New Guinea, all babies were given a BCG vaccine to prevent tuberculosis (TB). Babies in Canada do not normally get a BCG because there is not a lot of TB here.

As part of the military health screening, soldiers are routinely tested for TB by a Mantoux test when they join. Because of the BCG, Nichola reacted positively to the Mantoux test, and was immediately put in isolation for suspected TB.

I had to find documentation to show that Nichola had had a BCG vaccination before the authorities would allow her back in the barracks to continue the program.

When we saw her 6 weeks later, she no longer slouched when she walked. Her hands were always by her side and she was as fit as I had ever seen her. We took her out to dinner but she couldn't stay long as she had to get ready for the passing out parade the next day.

We watched in amazement. The military had taken a group of high school graduates and turned them into soldiers in 6 weeks. We had a little time after the ceremony to visit but then they were all put on the bus and travelled to Kingston and the Royal Military College of Canada (RMC).

Tim and I and Nichola's sisters drove from Antigonish to Kingston at the end of September 1998 to watch Nichola participate in the Obstacle Course. It marked the end of her first year orientation period and her start at RMC as an officer cadet.

We were all excited to see her and at one point, she marched past alongside but couldn't acknowledge us. We followed her around the thirteen obstacles. She started off wearing a yellow T-shirt with the other members of her squadron but after the second or third obstacle, there was so much mud, that everyone's T-shirt was brown.

In the evening, the parents were invited back to a squadron initiation. Each cadet was welcomed and the ending was the squadron singing Billy Joel's 'Goodnight Saigon'. I can still hear all those young voices singing the chorus:

And we would all go down together
We said we'd all go down together
Yes, we would all go down together.

I was teaching Grade 12 Sociology that year at Dr. J.H. Gillis Regional High School in Antigonish, the same high school that Nichola had graduated from the year before. I thought the students might be interested in hearing from Nichola.

We were doing a unit on rules societies use. Nichola talked about the rules at RMC. She explained that there was a Memorial Arch that you only walked under when you first arrived at RMC and not again, until your graduation day. One of the students asked her, "Don't you ever just go there at night and sneak through it?"

Nichola replied, "No, why would you?" And the student said, "Just to break the rule without getting caught," And Nichola just said, "No, you don't because it is important."

Nichola spent four years at RMC. She graduated with an honours degree in English, fully bilingual, and trained as an artillery officer. Her education was paid for, and she received a salary and contributed to her pension for all four years. In return, upon graduation, she promised to stay with the military for at least five years.

On graduation weekend 2002, Tim and I, her sisters, grandparents, and extended family watched her receive both her diploma and her commission as a 2nd Lieutenant. She was posted to the 1st Regiment Royal Canadian Horse Artillery in Shilo, Manitoba.

We had moved to Calgary by this time and we were thrilled that Nichola would be relatively close by. She talked to us about getting married at Christmas to another soldier whom she had met during basic training. We had met him many times over the four years and realized that they were not 'just friends' as she kept telling us.

Nichola was only 22 and I felt she needed time to establish her career before she got married. She then told me, "You're entitled to your opinion but I am getting married." And so she did, just after Christmas 2002.

Nichola was assigned to be part of Avalanche Control in Roger's Pass in early 2003. She stayed with us for a few days and I asked her to come and talk to my Grade 8 and 9 classes at the junior high school where I was teaching. She wore her green camouflage uniform and did countless push ups, some one handed, which impressed the boys.

There wasn't enough time for her to answer all the questions, so I had the students write to her and she responded with the following letter:

1 Apr 03

Dear Mum.

I'm sorry to be so long in getting back to you (and your classes), but as you know things have been really busy here. I am now in my last few days at AVCON (Avalanche Control), and thought that I would write your students back, hopefully answering their questions as I go.

My rotation was the last one of the year, so it has been the longest. We were here for a total of 6.5 weeks (22 Feb until 8 Apr).

It is the 1 April as I write this letter, and we have fired 372 rounds to date. We hope to go out at least twice more this week, bringing our total up to around 400. The most rounds that anyone has ever fired before are 649 ... so we aren't going to break that record this year. Unfortunately, the weather dictates how much we shoot, so there isn't much we can do. We have by far shot more than anyone else this year, though (the first rotation fired 32 rounds and the second 99).

I have been in charge of 12 people for the past 6 weeks. I organize the daily routine, the vehicle and gun maintenance, as well as the food that we eat, physical training, and any special activities that the guys* want to do. I have enjoyed being the one overall responsible, although it can be a bit stressful sometimes, too. It is a constant battle with the cook

* *guys*: Nichola usually called the soldiers in her command her 'guys', since that's what they were. However, there are—and obviously were!—women soldiers in the army as well, and as one commentator pointed out, this sort of unthinkingly gendered language is an example of what might be termed a 'micro-aggression': a little cut that doesn't seem very big in itself, but is part of a much larger systemic problem. In this book, therefore, I have tried to refer to Nichola's soldiers as soldiers, becuase that is first and foremost what they are, but we have left her words as they were written..

trying to get everyone fat and me trying to get everyone in shape.

I have an excellent group of soldiers, who are all motivated to have a good time so my job is pretty easy. We have organized trips to the Halycon Hot Springs, Revelstoke Brewery, tubing trips down Mount Fidelity (a huge 12 km mountain that we get pulled up in our tubes and then get to race down), and lots of snowshoeing, soccer, and ball-hockey. Plus, lots of shooting!

The daily routine looks something like this:

0700: Reveille

0730: Breakfast. I call the Avalanche Control Rep to find out if we are shooting that day. If we are, preparations start at 0800, and we are ready to shoot by 0900. If we are not shooting, the day continues like this:

0745:I give a briefing to the detachment about the day's activities

0800: GD (general duties) i.e. Cleaning the bathroom, common areas, etc.

0900: Ring maintenance (the rings are areas on the side of the highway where we deploy the guns. They have to be cleared of snow and debris each morning, so they are always ready for us to shoot). There are 18 positions, so clearing them usually takes the morning. One day, there was over 2 FEET of snow on all the positions. The guys were all the way at 12 (with only 6 to go), when the snowplough came and filled them all in again. That really sucked.

1200: Lunchtime

1300: Physical training for one group, the other usually goes to town for a rec run. Either myself or the Sgt (my 2I/C) is always here, in case we need to go shooting.

1600: The bar opens, everyone visits

1700: Supper

1800: Free time. We watch a lot of movies, play computer/board games, etc.

On the weekend, I like to give the guys Sat and Sun off if I can. I still get up and find out if we are shooting, but they don't have to be up until 1200 on Saturday. On Sunday, there is no hard timings and everyone can spend the day doing what they want. Within reason. They can't go into town unless they clear it through me and we can't go wandering off for hikes and stuff (due to the avalanche threat). My big responsibility is to make sure that no-one goes crazy having to be up here for 6 weeks. I ensure that everyone goes into town at least once a week and that we do a variety of activities. It seems to be working thus far.

Shooting has been awesome. Sometimes, the avalanche comes so close that we get 'dusted'. That is when the snow and dust from the avalanche gets blown over us. It isn't the actual avalanche (or we'd be in trouble!) but it is close. We've been dusted 6 times, which ties us with the record. One more and we'll have the record. We have set one record so far – we fired 338 rounds in 4 days. Those were the days that the highway through Roger's Pass was closed in the middle of March. Apparently, it was the worst storm up here in the last 20 years. We got over 3 FEET of snow over those four days. It was crazy.

Some specific questions that were asked:

1. What is the scariest thing that you have ever done in the army?

I think that, for me, the scariest thing was rappelling during my basic training. I am really scared of heights so it terrified me. We tied our own harness, which sucked. I didn't want to go down because I didn't trust my knots and I was sure that it was game over for me. It was a 40ft wall, and the worst part was getting over the edge. Even then, my muscles were so tight, it hurt to move down the rope. The guy at the other end was a lifesaver – he pretty much lowered me the whole way (I later married him!).

I had never understood how people could wet their pants because they were scared ... but I think the only reason that I didn't was because I had gone to the bathroom before we went up the wall. It was awful, and I remember contemplating quitting. But I had already been through 7 weeks (out of 8) of my basic training, and it seemed like too much to throw away. So I did it. I still don't like heights, but I am a lot better than I used to be.

I know one thing for sure now: if I ever

can't do something, I'm the only one stopping me. If I could do that, anything is possible.

2. Are there a lot of women in the Army?

The short answer is no. The long answer is that there are some, and there are more every day. It is definitely not the right lifestyle for everyone (men or women), but I really don't believe that gender has anything to do with whether you can be a good soldier. I guess that I am a little biased. I've worked with women who have been 5'3, 100 something lbs, and carried more for longer than guys who were 6' something and 200 something lbs… so much of what makes you a good soldier is your attitude and heart. And how good a shot you are with your rifle, I guess.

3. Do you think there will be a World War 3? If you get called up to fight in it, would you go?

My opinion on the first question is just as valid as yours. I read the same newspapers and watch the same TV shows. I agree with the person who wrote this question when she said she hopes there is not one. A common perception is that soldiers WANT war. I certainly don't. But I also believe in protecting my country and my family. If I get called up to fight in any conflict, I will certainly go. It is my job, and, I feel, my duty. You might say that 'no-one could make you fight'. In that case, I suggest you don't join the Canadian Forces.

4. What kind of stuff do you do in the military?

Well, I do a lot of different things. I took second language training, and am now bilingual (English-French). I did my training as an artillery officer, and am now in charge of a gun position (6 guns) in Shilo. I organize the training of approximately 100 soldiers, making sure that they get to go on different courses and get the qualifications they need to do their jobs well. I also get to come up here to AVCON, where I get to control avalanches. Basically, I get to do a lot of really cool stuff.

5. Even though it would be scary, are you kind of excited to go and defend your country?

Yes. It would be really scary … but also really awesome to go and do what I have been training to do. Not everyone thinks we should have a military, but when I think of my family and friends – I am very proud that I could help protect them or another family like them if there was a need.

6. Can you have pets where you live now?

Yes. I have a wonderful dog named Sam. Don't ask my parents about him, because they have a slightly different impression. I think Sam is perfect, and we have a great time together. He is a Lab X just about everything under the sun, and I love him to bits.

7. Does it cost money to buy your uniform?

Yes it does, but not my money. The military pays for all our uniforms/military equipment.

8. Will your rank ever improve? How?

Yes, it will improve, Just like you have different skills that you have to master before you can pass from one grade to another, there are different criteria for each rank in the military. I will (hopefully) be promoted to a Lieutenant in May.

9. Can anyone beat you in pushups?

Many, many people including one of the guys in my Mum's class … especially in the tricep pushups. I was really impressed.

10. What are the ranks in the army?

Whew! This is a long one. In the NCM (non-commissioned member) world there are as follows (lowest to highest):

Private
Corporal
Master-Corporal
Sergeant
Warrant
Sergeant-Major
Chief Warrant Officer

In the Officer world:

Officer-Cadet
Lieutenant
Captain
Major
Lieutenant Colonel

Colonel
Brigadier-General
Major-General
Lieutenant-General
General

I think that answered all the questions. I want to add one thing: I was really impressed with the opinions that some of you expressed about the military and war in general. Some of you were very pro-military, others weren't. It is great that you were able to articulate your arguments and support them in a letter. We are living in scary times, and it is important to feel strongly about world events. I'd argue that the reason you have that freedom of thought and choice was because a lot of people before you thought the same way, and were willing to fight for their beliefs. Thanks for helping me remember why my job is so important.

Sincerely,
Nichola Goddard
2LT
A/GPO A Bty
1 RCHA

★★★

When Nichola was posted to Canadian Forces Base Shilo, she was sent to work with Parks Canada to provide avalanche control in the Roger's Pass area.

Those of you that have driven through there know that there are rings set in cement on either side of the highway. If you stop at one of the rings and look around, you will see a sign that looks almost like a railway crossing and behind the sign, a glacier. The crossed arms of the sign are how the artillery sets its aim. Glaciers move slowly but are in the same place year after year.

Every year Parks Canada monitors the snowfall and tells the soldiers which glacier has to be blown up before it causes an avalanche and blocks the highway or catches people in its path. The gun is then taken to the ring, the officer takes aim, and the gun is fired, and the glacier comes down.

On one particular day, Parks Canada decided that the glacier behind the hotel had to come down. It had not been touched for 25 years. They were worried if it got any bigger and broke away, the avalanche would block the highway. For the glacier to be brought down safely, both the road and traffic had to be stopped.

Nichola got her soldiers in position, got the gun in the ring, and looked through the viewfinder. She could see the railway cross but there was a small tree in the way. She sent one of her soldiers to cut it down. He was gone for a long time.

People got out of their cars and wandered up, trying to find out what was happening. All the public could see were 6 or 8 soldiers, standing around, doing nothing. Eventually, Nichola sent another soldier to investigate. He returned quickly and said, "Ma'am, you better come and see this."

Nichola followed the soldier. She ended up going down a hill before she saw the railway sign and the other soldier. What she thought was a small sapling was in fact, the tip of a much larger tree that was at least 25 years old. The soldier had a little hatchet and was trying desperately to cut it down. He didn't want to leave without the task being completed.

Nichola returned to the highway, got Parks Canada to take a chainsaw to the tree, and eventually blew up the glacier. Although she laughed about it afterward, the hardest part was trying to explain to those waiting in their cars why it was taking so long. I am sure that we all have many trees where only the tips are seen. It's so easy to be a critic when you don't see the whole picture.

Nichola returned to Shilo and her life there. She lived in married quarters on the base with her husband, 2 dogs, and 2 cats. In the summer of 2003, her regiment became part of Operation Peregrine and she was part of the group that was sent to British Columbia to fight forest fires.

She had had a pedicure before she left and had the calluses taken off her feet. As a result, she ended up with terrible blisters as she was helicoptered on a side of a mountain and had to walk down in single file, looking for 'hot spots'—smouldering stumps and roots—that the soldiers extinguished.

★★★

Nichola's training continued as she took courses and advanced from 2nd Lieutenant, to Lieutenant, and then Captain. She came to love the artillery and the big guns. There was nothing she liked better than going on field exercises – the longer, the better. She would telephone us and talk about her soldiers, her neighbours, and her friends.

Her immediate boss, Major Anne Reiffenstein, was a great mentor to Nichola. When Anne was reposted in the summer of 2005, Nichola gave her a copy of *Anne of Green Gables* by L.M. Montgomery.

Nichola had written the following in it:

> Ma'am,
>
> As one can never have too many books, I wanted to share Anne Shirley's story with you. Anne Shirley is an orphan who spends the majority of her life being moved between foster homes and generally trying to fit in. She is constantly accused of 'not being a boy!' Anne makes no apologies about her behavior and mixes tomboy stunts with purely feminine concerns about her hair (red!) and nose (long!). Throughout the whole story, Anne only once regrets that she was not a boy. At that time, Matthew says, "I'd rather have you than a dozen boys" (page 282). Anne has earned her place and proven her worth to all

she has met.

I wanted to give you this story to thank you for all the guidance and professional development that you have given me. You have allowed me to develop my leadership abilities while being proud of my gender. You have caused me to view being a woman as an asset – not a detriment to the team or to my profession.

I can only hope to inspire other women to persevere and take pride in their accomplishments as you have for me.

Thank you.
Nichola

Soon after, Nichola was sent to CFB Wainright to train for the Afghan mission. We all spent Christmas together with Tim's family in Wales. One afternoon, Nichola sat us down and explained what was going to happen.

I mentioned something about peacekeeping, and Nichola looked at me and said, "You need to understand this is peacemaking, not peacekeeping."

She had a map of Afghanistan and showed us where she would be going. She gave us preaddressed envelopes so that we could write to her. She told us that she had made a will.

That was the point when all of us in the room began to understand the dangers she would be facing.

We saw her one more weekend in January when she came to Calgary. I wanted to go to Shilo to wave her off but she wouldn't let any of us be part of that. She called it the crying room. Looking back, I think she didn't want to break down in front of her soldiers.

Afghanistan

2006

Nichola began sending letters—public letters to family and friends talking about Afghanistan and her role there. From this point onwards, we will let her words tell the story.

LETTER ONE

CAPT. NICHOLA GODDARD'S FIRST LETTER HOME:

Hello Everyone! Well, as you all know, I arrived safe and sound into Afghanistan on 1 Feb. 2006. It took us four days to fly here — quite an adventurous four days!

The Trip

The first stop was Trenton, Ont., where our plane got held up for four hours because of problems with the fuel tank. That got fixed and we finally left for Prestwick, Scotland. Upon arrival there, duct tape fell off and the fuel tank gave up completely. We ended up spending 36 hours in Prestwick. For those of you who haven't been there, there isn't a lot to do for a bunch of soldiers without civilian clothing who aren't allowed to drink or leave the immediate metropolis of Prestwick. Anyway, got our own rooms in a local hotel and, as usual, managed to have a good time. I had never been to Scotland and have decided that it would be lovely to go back and do some hikes.

From Scotland, we flew into Zagreb, Croatia. That was really different! It was fun to be somewhere completely different from the U.K. or North America. It made me realize that I really haven't seen much of the world (that I remember, Mum and Dad!). The stopover was only a couple of hours and we were ready to do the final big leg to Dubai, UAE.

Dubai was amazing. It was too bad that we arrived at a crazy time in the middle of the night (0200 local) ... the base is set up like a resort. Complete with mini-golf, movies, mini-bar, etc. Wow. Even at 0200 it was impressive. I need to highlight this because of the huge contrast to KAF (Kandahar Airfield). More on that in a minute. Oh, I should also mention that there were beautiful showers, air conditioning, heat when you needed it, and all the guys had their own rooms. The location seems amazing ... I can't wait to stop over there when we fly back.

As you know, I was pretty apprehensive about the trip into KAF. I knew that we were going to fly "tactically" and was a little concerned that I'd totally embarrass myself and throw up all over some of my soldiers. I'd never been in a Herc (the big planes that the military uses to lift heavy equipment and move personnel — Herc stands for Hercules). It was HUGE. They crammed in so much kit, it was amazing. They drove the tractors right onto the plane to drop off the crates with our kit in them. Then, we got on. I discovered that the reason they can fit so much stuff is because they cram the people all together in the smallest space possible. We sat in four rows, the centre two with our backs to each other, facing the other row. We had to sit with our legs alternating, because otherwise we didn't fit. The flight was three-and-a-half hours long. I didn't sleep much! The tactical flying part was pretty tame. The Pang Screamer prepared me well! No one from my flight threw up, which was nice. We arrived into KAF around 0830 local time.

The Camp

I need to emphasize that the camp is HUGE. It is about 16 km long and employs 5,000 civilians. There are about 7,000 troops here from many nationalities. I have seen American, Dutch, Romanian, and British troops so far. The Canadians aren't quite all here yet — they should finish arriving by the 3rd or 4th of Feb. The local Afghans get paid $1 day (US). Initially, they tried to pay them $3/day, but the workers kept on getting killed. I guess that the unemployed guys would ask for a job and be turned down. He'd then wait outside for the next guy to come in, then he'd shoot him. Unemployed guy would then walk in and ask for a job. After a couple of incidences, they lowered the salary.

It really makes you think.

The camp is separated into chunks, with each nationality organizing their camp the way they see fit. There are three kitchens spread around the camp, and you can eat in whichever one you are closest to. The food seems to be OK. There is a lot of deep-fried stuff, but an OK selection of salads and vegetables. I won't get fat, but I shouldn't starve, either. The hours are very flexible, so you can basically eat whenever you get hungry.

The bathrooms get their own paragraph. I thought that I was pretty realistic, but even I will emphasize that it is pretty bad. There are two cesspools in the camp where all the raw sewage is dumped and purified. Depending on which direction the wind is blowing, it can be quite strong. The guys in charge of it definitely deserve to be on that show The Worst Jobs Ever. We are about 300m from the closest bathrooms.

You walk into the room and there are 10 toilets, each surrounded by a curtain that never shuts the whole way.

We are about 500m from a row of porta-potties. Depending on my mood, I can choose company or not. The showers are about 1000m away, but they are great.

There is lots of hot water for the women's showers and the water pressure is great. The showers aren't coed, so don't worry, Dad. I guess the guys are usually out of running water; it sucks to be them, I guess.The camp was originally sand, but I guess that was pretty hard to walk on and got really dusty. Someone decided that laying down a bunch of gravel would be a better decision. I guess it is, but the result is that your feet always hurt from walking on the big gravel chunks. Plus, the danger of rolling an ankle is ever-imminent. I imagine it is like walking on the beach — I will get used to it.

There are a fair number of facilities spread about the camp. There is a Canada house, where I called Mum and Dad from. There are 10 phones right next to each other. There is a pretense of privacy given by the paper-thin boards that are put up between people. The ideal is to end up between two people speaking French, that way you don't get distracted by their conversations. The phones have the added benefit of being right next to the airstrip, so any planes taking off or landing cut out all conversation. They also get cut off periodically, so don't panic if I'm on the phone and it dies. I guess the wires are above ground, so they get tripped all the time by vehicles. There are also 10 computers there. My computer account is set up now (that is how I am e-mailing) ... I should emphasize that the 10 phones and 10 computers are for the 1,200 Canadian troops that are in KAF. So, I'll apologize ... for not calling/e-mailing often and for calling at weird times. The trick seems to be typing out the e-mail on my laptop, and then e-mailing it as an attachment. This way, I can write a lot more and not take up a lot of time on the Internet. I really don't like talking with all the people around, so I'll apologize now for being pretty quiet.

Other facilities include the gym, which I haven't been to yet but apparently is quite nice. There is also an American house, Dutch house, etc. I haven't visited those. There is a Subway and a Burger King on the American side ... there is also a huge U.S. department store that I haven't been to yet. I'm going to get the big tour this afternoon. I'll tell you all about it in my next letter.

What else? Oh, there is no power. There is power in the camp, but it hasn't been run to our tents yet. They expect it to take a couple of weeks. Right now, there is a communal building where we can recharge stuff. The downside is that you have to sit there while it recharges because theft is a problem. I'm glad that Jay got me the computer that re-charges in a much shorter amount of time.

I think that is it that I can think to tell you about the camp. Tonight, I will be meeting with the American unit that is currently working in our area — it will be interesting to hear all of their stories and get their take on the area.

The Area

Wow. I knew that we were going to be on a desert surrounded by mountains. I knew that it was going to be hot. I knew that there would be a lot of sand. I knew that we would be about an hour from the city. I didn't know that it would be so beautiful. It is kind of like cutting out a piece of southern Manitoba, filling it with sand and putting it in Canmore's location.

It is beautiful. The mountains seem close, but I know they are at least 50 km away. The air is very dry, which is lovely. Even when it's hot, it's a dry hot. I am very glad that we came in the winter, because it is not unbearable. I can't wait to get out to see more of the country. Tory — I will find you a great rock. I am going to start taking pictures today, and I will send them home as soon as I get a good collection.

The Mission

I know that I told you guys a fair bit of stuff before I left about where I will be working and what my routine will be like. Not too much has changed from that. I can't e-mail any details about where I'll be going or when. Nor can I tell you over the phone when I'll be in the camp or when I'll be gone. I'm sorry about that, because I know you all worry. But we need to be pretty secretive about it so that no one finds out ahead of time where we are going or when. I know that you all understand. I will keep a journal and tell you all when I get home. In the meantime, please understand when I am very vague!!

The Guys

I am in a small tent right now with nine other officers. There is about a foot between our cots, so it is pretty tight. This morning, I put my lock inside my combat boot. Then, I picked up my boots and yelled out "Scorpion check" as I tipped my boot upside down beside my buddy's cot. There was a big "thump" as the lock fell out. My buddy, Howard Han for those Shilo folk, shot out of bed like he'd been shot. It was pretty good. The good news is that I no longer need to worry about being the first one to scream like a little girl. Morale is pretty high, as we are all glad to finally be here. The last check was 196 days (give or take) until we come home.

I think of you all often and can't wait to see you all again. I hope that life on the home front is interesting as usual and that you are all remembering to smile.

Nich

★★★

LETTER TWO

WEEK TWO IN KANDAHAR

Hello Everyone,

I am writing from my bunk bed — we have moved up in the world and now live in a BAT (which stands for Big $$ Tent) which is pretty cosy. There are about 200 people in each tent. There is also power, which is awesome!!

I got a top bunk, so I'm happy. I haven't really had time to appreciate living inside a tent with power, though, because I have been so busy.

Overall, the quality of life in KAF is improving daily. The females now have their own bathroom, which is really nice. There's a lot to be said for having your own cubicle. Each bathroom/shower room has its own water supply. Because there are far fewer females, we always have hot water and lots of it. That is really nice, because the guys still complain about running out all of the time. I think I mentioned that in the last letter — but it's worth saying again.

I also bought a little mat for my feet in the morning. It covers up the big gravel chunks so it's not quite as bad to get off my bunk. The bunk beds are pretty little. My Sgt. is 6'4" and he has to sleep diagonally — Jay would hate it! They are also quite flimsy. I almost knocked mine over climbing in without the Sgt. down below to anchor me. We have a SOP (Standard Operating Procedure) established now so there haven't been any other incidents. My crew all gets to sleep right beside one another, which I really like. The only thing to really complain about is the smell. Two hundred men in one tent after a busy day rivals the cesspool outside. I don't think my nose hairs will ever be the same again.

I can't believe that we have been here for only a week. The days are all so full, time seems to fly by. On the other hand, you are never far from my thoughts. I got a letter from Victoria today (thanks! My first one). It was great to have news from home. I find that I am very cut off from the outside world. I have absolutely no idea what is going on outside of Afghanistan and even my knowledge of Afghanistan is very restricted to the Kandahar area. So — any news articles or stories would be really appreciated.

My crew is doing really well. Our morale is pretty high and we are keeping very busy. It is an amazing feeling to get out and actually do our job. I knew that we were well trained, but I didn't realize quite how well until we started actually doing road moves and patrols. I am very confident in my crew and in our equipment. Don't worry Dad, confidence does not equal carelessness. We are very careful. I find our trips "out of the wire" very tiring mentally. We are all keyed up and super alert for the whole thing, so we're all really tired when we get back. But, it is great to get out there and see the country.

Leaving KAF (Kandahar Airfield) is like moving to another world. First, we cross about 2 km of garbage. The field of garbage always has people "shopping" as Mum would say. It is quite sad. There are a couple of apartment buildings that have half collapsed. When you get to the other side, you see that they don't have a back at all. Apparently, they were hit by 500 lb. bombs sometime ago. They are filled with people. The kids all run out to watch us drive by. Sometimes they wave and smile, but other times they swear at us and throw rocks. I still find it pretty shocking to see young children so full of hate at us being here. But others wave and smile and seem to want us around. It is hard to know who is right. I just have to believe that we are doing a good thing, especially when I hear our intelligence updates about the widespread violence and I see the terrible poverty.

I have seen several herds of wild camels. I'm still trying to find a tame one so that I can go for a ride. I think that must be one of those "gotta do it" things. The opportunity hasn't come up yet, but I'm only in week two. Other bizarre things — the donkeys are hobbled. Their front legs are tied so close together that they can't even walk, they have to hop. Gundy would be horrified. I found it very sad to watch. On the other hand, these people have so little, it is easy to understand that they don't want their only donkey to run away.

I can't begin to describe the poverty that I have seen here. It actually makes me sick to my stomach to see how little these people have. In the countryside, there are lean-tos made out of old tarp and almost see-through cloth. It seems like dozens of people fit into them. We went to practise shooting our weapons and the locals all gathered around to watch.

That was fine, but as soon as we were done, they came to scavenge ... they collected all of the used casings from our weapons. They were actually pushing and shoving each other to get at it.I have also never seen so many people maimed and wounded. People with crutches and people without who should have them.

I have seen about 100 men in our trips and easily double that in children, but no women so far. I don't think they realize that I am a woman when we drive by, which is fine by me.

I can see why people dream about visiting here. It is stunningly beautiful in areas. I got to see the red desert to the south — it was amazing. I don't think any description or photo could do it justice. It was silhouetted on both sides by the mountains to the east, and the plains to the west. It stretched south for as far as we could see. It wasn't flat, like the deserts in the movies. Instead, it was rolling and a blood red colour. The sand was so fine, you couldn't even pick it up. I will find you a cool rock, Tory, don't worry!

So far, my most interesting stories involve the insects and animals that I have seen. Still no camel spiders or scorpions, but I did see a wild stick bug — it looked just like they look at the zoo. It must have been a baby one, though, because it was very small. We've also seen some pretty cool lizards and spiders, but all small. I've got to say, I'm not really disappointed.

It has been getting steadily hotter. It reaches about 35 C in the afternoons, but drops down to about 5 C at night. As soon as the sun goes down, the temperature drops completely. I am definitely working on my tan!! We have air conditioning in our vehicle, which is awesome. Anything without our vehicle sucks more than I could ever describe. My personal protective equipment weighs about 40 lbs., plus the weight of a rucksack (between 40-60 lbs.) . . . that is two-thirds of my body weight and I feel every pound of it. "Living the dream" as we all say. I've got to admit, the LCF (look cool factor) is pretty good. I will take lots of pictures.

I guess that is it — hopefully, the weeks continue to fly by. I trust that all is well on the home front. I miss you guys.

Nich

★★★

LETTER THREE

WEEK THREE IN KANDAHAR

Week three seemed to fly by. Just one more week and we'll be one month down, five to go. Really four to go, because one month is dedicated to leave.

Exciting details from this week included the final arrival of the remainder of our military kit. We also received an air hockey table for our BAT (Big J$$ Tent, for those who missed letter 2) that is located about five feet from my bed. It makes for a great sleeping environment. Fortunately, I am usually so tired that sleeping is not a problem!

We still haven't gotten our UAB (unaccompanied baggage). Apparently, it's in the camp but they won't give it to us until all of the ROTO 0 guys leave. No one is sure why that is, but there is a big lottery going around as guys pick days when it will arrive. I have laid my dollar for March 5th. We'll see if I'm right.

Week Three is marked by a series of small yet critical events:

1. The complete and total disappearance of all toilet paper in our area of the camp. This resulted in raids onto other camps and good PR statements such as "the Americans don't really use it anyway." The fallout of this event is that we are now no longer allowed to cut through the other camps on our way to the kitchen or canteen. People are going to be talking about "The great TP shortage of 2006" for months to come ... tensions were pretty high for a while. We have since been restocked. Now the big concern is about hoarding. I must confess to have my own stash in case of a repeat emergency.

2. Wed night was the first karaoke night that I've made it to. It turns out that my sergeant is a hidden karaoke superstar.

He wouldn't get up in front of the crowd, though. In case you're curious, I didn't either (there are advantages to it being a dry camp).

3. My HLTA was moved from April to June. June seems like a long way away, but I think Jay is happy that he'll have more uninterrupted study time. It is nice that I'll be missing one of the hottest months and also that I'll only have a month to go at that point. I just hope that the next four months continue to fly by.

4. I saw my first Afghani woman. She was in a full burka and walking back from the gas station/bus stop. I don't know how they can see or function. I can't imagine never feeling the sun on my face or not really being able to see where I'm going. Imagine not being able to go out for a run or a relaxed walk! Then I remind myself that these people are primarily concerned with survival — they would never waste energy on a run or go for a relaxed walk, there is enough walking to the nearest water source! I remind myself to be open-minded; we have some pretty whacked cultural idiosyncrasies, too.

5. A "female quarters" was established

within our BAT. It is sectioned off by tarp so that we are completely isolated from the males. Personally, I think that we have taken a benign situation and created a fantasy. The original intent was to move us to a completely different BAT. I wrote a memorandum protesting the move to the Commanding Officer. He actually wrote back to me personally, and agreed to compromise but wanted us in a segregated cell. I guess it is OK. Girls generally smell better than guys and I get my own bunk now so I'm not complaining too much. It is more for when the imbedded media arrive, the female reporters might be uncomfortable, I guess. Mind you, both of my roommates are open lesbians, so I think that my chances of being gawked at are actually higher now. It's all good.

6. We received a huge crate of books and magazines donated by helpful Canadians for the troops overseas. When the box was first opened, there was a huge line to get a book. It quickly dissipated. The donations included almost the entire Harlequin Romance series, the majority of Danielle Steel's novels and Canadian women's magazines. I'm sure

they were sent with the best of intentions but they didn't really meet with the soldiers' idea of what is "cool."

On a more serious note, on Tuesday we attended the "ramp" ceremony for the four U.S. soldiers that were killed by an IED this week. It was quite moving. A "ramp" ceremony is where they hold a huge parade and the soldiers' coffins are loaded up the ramp onto the plane heading home. Soldiers from the deceased's unit line the route from the vehicle delivering the coffin to the plane. The coffins were carried by fellow section members and friends. The rest of us, close to 5,000 strong, formed up along the runway and saluted them as they were carried onto the plane. It was short, very serious, and terribly sad.

I hope that it was my last one.

My crew continues to do really well. We have our vehicle sorted out and have been working on crew drills. Tonight we're having a "party pizza night" which I'm pretty excited about. The food here is OK, but it is repetitive and usually pretty greasy. I find that I crave steamed (as opposed to stewed) vegetables. Still, anywhere that you can order pizza delivered to the "Canadian Camp, second BAT to the East," is pretty cool. I sure miss Bubu's quiches and soups, though!!!

I have started to get mail now, which is awesome. Every day this week I've gotten a letter. I will write individual responses to them all, but e-mail is a much faster way of getting the weekly message out. It makes me feel so much closer to home — thank you for everyone who has made the effort to send mail. For those of you who haven't, don't feel too guilty. I'm just sitting here on my bunk bed, smelling a wonderful combination of sweaty feet and sewage, thinking of home ... no need to write, sniff! Sniff!

Seriously — life here is great. I think that we have more amenities than I remember having in Black Lake and the heat hasn't been too unbearable. We're going to be doing some dismounted stuff in the future that will suck, but I should come away with some good pictures and great stories.

I hope that you are all doing well and will write again next week.

Nich

★★★

LETTER FOUR

WEEK FIVE

Hello All,

I am afraid that this week's letter will be neither long nor particularly cheerful. There is a lot to say, but most of it is pretty serious and depressing. But, you are all in with me for good or for bad, so I'll launch into this week.

This week started off quite slow. My crew and I went out for a couple of routine patrols around the area. They were uneventful. We got to fire off some mortar rounds at one of the ranges and generally had a good time being gunners.

Early this week, I attended my second American ramp ceremony. The service was virtually identical to the first one, except that it was emotionally much harder because the feeling that this wasn't going to be the last one was unavoidable. I'm not sure exactly how many American soldiers have been killed in theatre (between here and Iraq), but I know that it is in the mid-2,500s ... it was difficult to accept how matter-of-fact they were about the whole thing. It was also harder because this time it dealt with a normal soldier, just like us. The time before it had been for American special forces guys — it is easy to think of them as different from "us." But this soldier was just like any one of us, and it was horrible. I was in the first row behind the American troops that were lining the route, and I could hear a couple of them crying. That was really tough.

Two days later, we attended the first Canadian ramp ceremony held in theatre. This time, it was a soldier that I had lived near and worked with in Shilo. This time, I knew the pallbearers, and I was one of the soldiers lining the route. Our service was longer than the American one, but I found it very moving. The casket was driven onto the parade, and soldiers from his section acted as pallbearers. The four Canadian Padres serving in theatre said a brief blessing and short prayer, and the procession moved onto the plane. I ask that your thoughts and prayers go with the young man's family. He is survived by his wife and two young daughters.

This week was also notable in the several IED strikes and confirmed rocket attacks against coalition vehicles/convoys. Overall, it was a very emotional and high-stress week.

I don't want you to feel that I am depressed or defeated. Far from it. The longer that we are in theatre and the more that we actually interact with the Afghan people, the more I feel that we are serving a purpose here. I think that these people, through the Afghan National Army and Afghan National Police, are trying to achieve something that we in Canada have long since taken for granted. They lay down their lives daily to try to seize something that is so idealistic it is almost impossible to define. It goes beyond women wearing burkas and children being taught to read and write. The Afghan people have chosen who will lead them.

Their new government is striving to make Afghanistan a better place. I had never truly appreciated the awesome power of a democratic government before. We are here to assist that legitimate and democratically elected government. It is easy to poke holes in that statement and say that the system is corrupt and that violence and poverty make people easy targets for our own agendas. Those statements are true; however, we have to start somewhere. With the best of intentions, we have started in Afghanistan. There is nowhere else that I'd rather be right now.

Nichola

★★★

LETTER FIVE

WEEKS SIX TO EIGHT

25 March 2006

Hello Everyone,

I am afraid that this letter will be a long one, so go and get a coffee (Tim Hortons if you can swing it; I really miss my Single Singles) and pull up a chair. There is so much to say, I am not even sure where to begin. The good news is that you can feel free to skim if your eyes start to glaze over.

I just got back from Operation Sola Kowel (Pashtu for Peacemaker). I was deployed north of Kandahar city for the last two weeks. It was an incredibly challenging and rewarding experience. I feel like a poster child for why people should join the military — it was an amazing 15 days.

We did not stick to any type of routine, as hard as that may be to believe for those who know me well. One of the biggest challenges here is trying not to set a pattern. The local informant system is better than any CSIS network imaginable, so we try not to give them any more help than necessary. We make sure that patrols always go out at unpredictable intervals and that our routes change at bizarre places. This is not as challenging as it sounds, as a vehicle breakdown (very common) or road on the map that doesn't actually exist (happens all the time) force us to change our timings and routes frequently. The big joke is that there is no way for the bad guys to guess our next move, because we aren't sure yet, either. One of those "funny because it's true" statements.

Anyway, our mission was to move into isolated areas, either by foot or with our vehicles to meet with the local elders and conduct shirras. Shirra is the Pashtu word for "meeting" or what we are calling "leader engagements." Essentially, a group of 30-50 soldiers shows up on the outside of town. A smaller delegation of five-to-10 soldiers and three-to-five Afghan National Army (ANA) soldiers (depending on the size of the town) goes forward under the remainder's watchful eye. They ask to speak to the village leader and/or elders. In every village that we visited (I lost track after 10), this was absolutely no problem. A group of three-to-10 men would show up, with one designated leader. They would sit down somewhere in the open, watched by the remainder of the men in the village. We would watch our emissaries very closely for security reasons. Then, the shirra would begin. In most of the villages, after about 10 minutes of pleasantries, the chai (sweet tea) and bread would be brought out. They would also bring out candy and sometimes soup. Then, the real business would begin.

I was honoured to be invited to two different shirras. I really thought that the whole female thing would be a huge issue. It was, but not in the way that I thought it would be. The first time, it was an ANA commander who insisted that I be included. It was not that my leadership was excusing or excluding me — as an artillery officer, I was set in a position of overwatch doing my job ... the infantry officers were involved in the actual shirra. Anyway, I had to climb down from my precarious perch on the side of a mountain to drink chai. I am not sure how serious the discussion was before I got there, but once I arrived it quickly centered on my marriage status. The big shock was not that I was in the army, but that I was married and in the army. The fact that my husband was not also a soldier was even more disturbing (don't worry, Jay, I said that if you were strong enough to handle me, you didn't need to be a soldier, too.) The remainder of the discussion revolved around my inexplicable lack of children. The elder offered to go inside and get me some milk and bread, as diet was probably the issue. He was 67 and had two wives and several children under the age of 10 ... I said that my husband would definitely say that one wife was enough. He thought that was hysterical, and I was a hit.

The second shirra that I was invited to was quite large. About 15 elders turned up with close to 20 children. We are always relieved to see children, as it means that the meeting will probably go smoothly. Anyway, here the issue was not my lack of children, but my availability. My boss was apparently asked if I was available to marry one of the elder's sons who looked to be about 15. After we'd established that I was already married, the issue turned to the all-important one of baking bread. When I confessed that I could not make the delicious flat bread that they serve (like a flat naan bread) the elder asked, "Can you at least boil water to make chai?" I was quite indignant in my response "Yes!!" which amused them all.

Working with the ANA and interpreters was eye-opening, to say the least. I am always astonished at the way that the military acts as a great equalizer. It doesn't matter where you are from, or how much money you had growing up or the size of your family. It doesn't even matter what country you're from or your level of education. Once you're out with other soldiers, doing your thing, we are all the same. We respect each other based on ability, not background. We value a positive attitude, determination, and a good sense of humour.

The ANA possessed all of those qualities to a high degree.

The ANA soldiers are very professional and very competent. They are also in amazing physical shape. Watching them run up and down the mountains with all of their gear was phenomenal. Seeing how proud they are of their country and how determined they are to work towards peace was inspiring. They are paid very little and do very dangerous work — it is not rhetoric for them. They really do want to get rid of the Taliban and al-Qaida to make their country a better place.

The interpreters are even more idealistic. They are paid quite well by local standards, but many of them risk their lives by coming out with us. Some don't want to go into specific areas, because of past family conflicts. One interpreter was born in Afghanistan, but his family fled to Pakistan in the mid-'70s. He came here two years ago to be an interpreter, as he feels it is his way to help Afghanistan. He spoke Farsi, Pashtu and English without any problems at all.

I think that my proudest moment over the last 15 days was after a 10 km march with a 2,000 foot altitude gain. I was carrying approximately 100 lbs. of kit. It was a lot. It was the most physically challenging thing that I have ever done — and I've done some crazy stuff. There were two points where I almost gave up. After we had done the climb up, and were coming down through the valley, one of the ANA soldiers came up to me with an interpreter. The interpreter said, "They want me to tell you that all of the ANA are talking about you, because you have done this march with us." I said, "Tell him that I am talking about them, because they can run up and down the mountains." After this message was translated, the ANA soldier came up to me and said in broken English (better than my Pashtu): "I fight Taliban. I fight al-Qaida. You fight also. Dersi. Mananna" (Dersi is Pashtu for "very good" and Mananna is Pashtu for "thank you").

Another proud moment: we were in a village and were just getting on our kit to walk to the next town.

I had attracted a crowd of five men aged 15-60 who were watching me. It is kind of funny, I can sort of see why the Afghan women cover up their faces. The men are pretty bold. I am not sure how I am going to feel walking through a town without attracting a crowd — it will be quite humbling after all of the attention that I am getting here.

A man that must have been at least 60 came over to help me put on my rucksack. He almost took a knee lifting it up, but he did it. It was really neat.

Anyway, the interpreter came up and had a two-, three-minute conversation in Pashtu with the five men who were watching me. Then he turned to me and said, "Please excuse their staring. They are just very surprised that you are a woman working with all of these men. I have told them that you climbed over the mountain with us with your heavy bag and that you had no problems. They think that you must be very strong. I explained to them that you are just like the men, and that you can do everything that they can do the same as them."

It was perhaps the greatest statement of equality that I have ever heard — and it was given by a Pakistani-raised, Afghan male in the middle of an Afghan village that is only accessible by a five km walk up a mountain. It just goes to show that anything is possible and that stereotypes are often completely wrong.

A few other highlights that I should mention. Last week was the Afghan New Year. I, along with about 15 other people, was invited to the Afghan National Army New Year's celebration while we were out. They slaughtered three goats in celebration. I'd never had goat before. It tasted sort of like chicken ... just kidding. It was actually quite good. They roasted it over an open fire and served it wrapped in the flat naan-style bread. Then there was the soup. The soup was like a chicken broth except that it smelled and tasted like you had just dug the goat up from under a rock. I was lucky enough to get an extra serving of fat in mine. Wow. The only thing that I can even remember tasting as bad was the dead seal that we had in the N.W.T ... and that had been left decomposing for days. It was completely disgusting. I don't know where I got the intestinal fortitude to finish it off, but I drank my cup without making a face or anything. It took about 12 hours for me to get rid of the taste, though. Ugh. Talk about memories that I'll never forget.

I keep thinking about my grandparents, and what they must have gone through in World War I and II. This is nothing compared to that. I have an end-date. I know that I'll be home sometime in August. I have the ability to come back to a warm tent and call home to hear my Mum's voice. I have the ability to check e-mail and send a message instantly. I am so proud of all of the veterans that I know, but especially both of my grandfathers and grandmothers. I am in such good company in uniform. It truly is an honour to be wearing a uniform overseas.

What I want to talk about is the importance of family and friends. I think of you often, especially when

I see especially different or funny things. When I got back there was a stack of mail. I'm not kidding. Like, over 25 envelopes. I've written back to about half of the people now, and hope to get through the rest of the letters tomorrow. It means so much to me that so many people have taken the time to e- mail/write/mail newspapers and letters.

Thank you.

Home sometimes feels very far away. Especially when it is Saturday night and we have deep fried catfish at the mess, because our mess is an American one and they eat some strange stuff ... your letters make me feel that much closer. Thank you.

Finally, I ask that you all think, pray, meditate, whatever it is that you believe works about Capt. Trevor Greene, the soldier who was attacked by an axe at a shirra several weeks ago and seriously injured. His condition remains serious but stable. Please think of his family and of him. He is an excellent person.

Nichola

★★★

LETTER SIX

WEEKS NINE THROUGH TWELVE

May 3, 2006

Hello All,

I am feeling a certain amount of performance anxiety as I sit to write the latest letter ... I have received so much positive feedback from the other letters, I don't want this one to be a disappointment. I know that I have been gone for a while, so I will try to recount the last month's activities as accurately as possible. On the 29th March, a soldier from Charlie Company, the infantry company that I work with, was killed in action in a forward operating base (FOB). Three others were injured.

The ramp ceremony was especially moving, as it was the first time in a long while that a Canadian has been killed overseas in a firefight. I was in the front rank, standing beside the three injured soldiers as we saluted someone who epitomized everything that Canadians in Afghanistan represent. Private Costall was killed in a firefight, defending the

FOB from over 100 Taliban soldiers. The gate that he died defending has since been renamed, "Costall Gate."

Three days after Private Costall's death, my party with the remainder of Charlie Company moved into the forward operating base (FOB) to assist in its defence. We were told that we would be going for one- to-seven days. Twenty-nine days later, we came back to KAFJ. This latest letter will be about my time in the FOB.

Although the FOB is not physically that far from KAF, it took us 30 hours to reach it. We had intended to leave at first light from KAF, but the powers that be conspired against us, and we had a hard time tracking down all of the interpreters, medics, etc., that are "must haves" prior to rolling out of the wire.

Finally, we were ready to leave ... just in time for the Sunday afternoon market in Kandahar city. Our vehicle convoy was huge, almost 50 vehicles. To make it a little more manageable, we left in five packets of eight-10 vehicles. I was in the second packet.

Just prior to my packet hitting Kandahar city (or KC, for those who are in the know), packet 1 hit and killed a donkey. They were unable to properly secure the area, so they pushed on, directing packet 3 to deal with the donkey and owner. My packet took a different route. I can't quite describe what it is like moving our huge armoured vehicle through a city teeming with people, kids, donkeys, dogs, carts, shops, and cars on streets that are designed for small cars. To mitigate the risk of suicide bombers cutting between our vehicles, we drive very close together and move quite quickly. My hat goes off to our drivers — mine kept us within five feet of the vehicle in front for the hour that it took us to drive through the city; amazing.

Anyway, just prior to my packet getting out of the city, packet 4 discovered that they had taken a wrong turn and were now about halfway up a one-way street, going the wrong way. To make matters worse, packet 4 was made up of the guns and gun trucks ... about 70 feet in length per truck. There were two of them, plus the other vehicles in their packet. A three-point turn was not an option! I was impressed by the lieutenant who came over the radio and said, very calmly, "Um. We seem to be going the wrong way up a one-way street. We are trying to convince the traffic in front of us to turn around. Any security you could send us would be appreciated." That took about an hour to sort out. In the meantime, my packet was stopped on the edge of KC ... not a great place to be. That was when the intelligence hits reporting a suicide bomber in a white Toyota Corolla heading our way started to get sent in.

As we knew we were going to be stopped for a while, we pulled over to the side of the road, and started marshalling vehicles. They had to be quickly searched and then allowed to pass through. KC has a LOT of vehicle traffic, and we were trying to do a thorough job without holding up people ... a big traffic backlog is the worst PR move ever, as you big city readers can appreciate. After about 10 minutes, we realized that we had pulled over in front of a boys' orphanage. There were about 100 boys of all ages outside, ostensibly playing soccer. I couldn't count the number of times they kicked the ball over the wall and had to come out to get it, en masse. It is funny to me that boys are boys, no matter where you are.

Anyway, as the threat of suicide bombers continued to escalate, every second car seemed to be a white

Toyota Corolla with one person in it and suspicious packaging in the back. Everyone remained calm, and once again, I was amazed at the professionalism of our soldiers. We had been moving traffic for about an hour when Packet 4 eventually met up with the rest of our convoy ... only to discover that one of their vehicles was incapable of going more than five km/hour ... recovery had to be called.

Packet 3 had also met up with us at this point, after unsuccessfully trying to locate the dead donkey and owner. I'm not sure why the guy wouldn't have stuck around for two hours, waiting for more military people to show up and question him about his donkey ... although I understand why we can't just pay off guys when stuff like this happens, it makes the remuneration process very long and frustrating for everyone involved. Recovery arrived about an hour later for the downed vehicle, and then we were ready to roll.

We had moved about 20 minutes outside of KC when the next incident happened. You have probably all seen pictures of the LAVs and the cannon on the front? Well, we have the ability to traverse the cannon in all directions. When we are driving, we usually alternate sides that we are pointed at, to maximize coverage. For example, my vehicle will take from 12 o'clock to three o'clock. The vehicle behind will take from 12 o'clock to nine o'clock, etc. Anyway, one of the LAVs passed too close to a truck, hitting the truck. Fortunately, the truck was static, and no one was in the front of it. The turret was knocked right around, hitting the two soldiers standing in the back. Both were seriously injured and were sent back to Canada for reconstructive surgery — but both will be OK. The high point of that was the one guy with a smashed in jaw, concussion, broken nose, and serious whiplash who said to the medic, "Doc, my head really hurts." To which the medic replied, "no $H!T, buddy." They were airlifted out, and will both be OK.

We were then ready to carry on ... oh!

I should mention at this point that I then saw my first honest-to- goodness unmarked minefield. It really wasn't that exciting. It is hard to believe that such small and inanimate things can cause such pain and destruction. The mine was an anti-tank mine, and definitely off of the road, so it didn't cause us any difficulty.

At this point, we were ready to carry on. We stopped to refuel, and then began our last 30km cross- country portion around suppertime. We thought it would take us about three hours. 15 hours later, we rolled into the FOB.

Why did it take so long, you may ask ... well, let me tell you.

We were going cross country, which wasn't too bad. The area was hard-packed sand with rolling hills, and was quite easy to drive on. It was just getting dark as we started, so we had to slow down a fair bit when it got dark. We were driving without any lights, using our thermal and night vision devices to see. It worked OK. We had been going about an hour when someone realized that we had lost a vehicle. As in, it had completely disappeared off the face of the planet. To make it even more bizarre, it was a big truck about the size of a semi-trailer that we had "lost." We started to look for it, and ended up getting two helicopters to come and help us to a search. Two hours later, we found it. I guess that when everyone else turned left, these guys turned right. They then drove off a 10 foot drop, where they scared the crap out of themselves. As perhaps anyone would do in this moment of crisis, they then turned off the engine and all the lights, and sat in their vehicle, waiting for help ... finally, we found them.

As we started to move forward again, the vehicle in front of me hit a huge hole, scaring the crap out of their driver. Their communications gear was also knocked out. They stopped and sat there. This might sound stupid to you, but please keep in mind that we had been traveling through pretty stressful ground for about 20 hours now, and tempers were wearing a little thin. As everyone who knows me well can attest to, I am quite patient and understanding of indecisiveness in others, especially when I am tired and hungry and just want to get to the end point. I must confess to using words that would shock my parents as I climbed out of my vehicle to go and sort out the vehicle in front of me. It was at this point that we started seeing the tracer fire ...

My sergeant started to yell at me to "get in the f*c!ing vehicle," as I was busy yelling at the vehicle in front of us to start "your f*c!ing vehicle" ... Anyway, what the tracer fire didn't do for the vehicle in front, my-ah-words of encouragement seemed to do the trick, and they started up. The tracer fire really wasn't aimed at us, so that was OK ... we think it was likely being used as a way of signaling between the villages that we were en route. Anyway, no one was hurt by it, which is the important thing. We carried on ...

Finally, we arrived at the FOB — which is where the adventure truly begins.

I can't talk about the security of the FOB, or its exact location, or its name. But I can tell you that when the 150 of us showed up, there were two toilets. Oh, the toilets were also communal (ie., No walls around them) ... that was it for amenities. The toilets were also like the ones in Jarhead, where some unfortunate soul gets to burn the contents of the bucket once a day. Needless to say, a high priority for everyone was to build more toilets. They were completed by the third day there, which was awesome. Showers came about two weeks later, as we settled into the realization that we were there for the long haul.

The area itself was beautiful and the wealthiest area that I have seen yet in Afghanistan. Houses had basements and some even had second storeys. Some would not have looked out of place in downtown Brandon, (Man.); it was amazing. Most houses had electricity, virtually every house had a generator and reliable water source. I saw my first poppy fields, and was amazed at how beautiful they are. They also don't look anything like the poppies that we wear on Remembrance Day, in case you were curious.

They grow like tulips, very tall and very straight with big flowers. Not that I am an expert, but I can now tell you which ones produce the best heroin ... it was an interesting few weeks!

It was a lot warmer in the FOB then

back in KAF. It got up to 57 C at one point — I kept on telling myself that it was a "dry hot," but I'm not sure how much that helped. I think that the worst was that we had no way of freezing anything. We were drinking bottled water, but by lunchtime, it would be at least 50 C ... you were so thirsty, you had to drink, but it was almost too hot to drink. Crazy. We experimented with keeping it in the shade, in a wet sock ... but it was still gross, warm water.

Two high points that are worth mentioning at this time. We had been there about two weeks when a team of specialists came up from KAF to check out the area. They flew in by chopper (no 30-hour road move for them!). The officer asked me how I was finding things; I said that they were pretty good as we now had showers. I pointed with pride to the four-stall shower booth that the engineers had built for us. The officer said, "Wow, that would be amazing. Do you have a towel that I can borrow?" I stared at him in stunned disbelief, and then responded, "Buddy, I came out here with four sets of clothes. I have been here for 20 days, and I don't know when I'm going back to KAF. Even if I had a towel, I wouldn't let you use it." I didn't see him again after that.

Another high point — we were on hard rations throughout, which is about as exciting as it sounds. Anyway, we had been there about two weeks when a couple of Americans came over. They had a refrigerating unit with them. Apparently, they had thawed out some steaks, but they had thawed "way more than they could eat." They wanted to know if we wanted any. We, of course, said yes ... they were delicious! I don't think that I've ever had steak that good.

The trip back was, if anything, longer and more exciting than the trip out. I won't go into all the details ... basically, take the trip out but add a couple more serious vehicle breakdowns and an IED strike that didn't hurt anyone, double the length ... and three days later we were back All in all, quite a month.

Nichola

★★★

That was Nichola's last public letter. We have another facet of her time if Afghanistan courtesy of Lisa LaFlamme, currently the chief anchor and senior editor of CTV National News. In March 2006, Lisa LaFlamme spent 12 days embedded with Nichola and her soldiers. Here is a transcript of an interview she did with Nichola. It was never aired on television.

LISA LAFLAMME:

How much do you expect this [mission] to test your limitations?

NICHOLA:

I think every mission does. This will be my crew's 13th time out of the wire in the last six weeks. It doesn't really matter if you're going out for a couple of hours or a couple of weeks, you do all the same stuff and face all the same stressors. At the same time, it's exactly the same thing we've been doing for the last 6 weeks we've been here.

LISA LAFLAMME:

It's also really an uncharted territory up there where we are going.

NICHOLA:

I got the chance to go up and do what

they call a leader's recee. I've been probably three - quarter's of the way up but this will be the first time for my crew to be up that far so it will be good. It's always an adventure.

LISA LAFLAMME:

How do you prep for something like this? The insurgency is so unpredictable. How do you prepare for that?

NICHOLA:

What I focus on with my guys is, I make up the statistic, but there's a probably 25% of what we can effect. We can effect that by knowing our drills, knowing how we're going to react to things, knowing that we know our job, and then 75% is just reacting to it. So, there's very little we can actually control once we roll out of here, so the stuff we can, we take positive control of, and the other stuff, we just do what we do best and react to it.

LISA LAFLAMME:

Does it go through your mind what happened last Saturday at the shura? [Captain Trevor Greene was axed on March 4, 2006 while talking with community elders.]

NICHOLA:

Oh, yeah, it does all the time cause I hope we catch the guys. It's brutal. I think we think about that all the time, just the importance of watching our own back and watching out for each other.

LISA LAFLAMME:

So, no trepidation for you personally?

NICHOLA:

Not in that sense of reacting to stuff. I think everyone hopes they make the right call where they're put in that position so you can't do much more than that I guess.

LISA LAFLAMME:

So, if not in that sense, then in what sense do you personally have concerns, fears even?

NICHOLA:

My big concern is for my crew, so I guess the big pressure is on me. If I make a call and it's the wrong call, I won't know that till I do it, then just hope for the best – for me that's my biggest concern. I know that my guys know what to do so I don't have any worries there.

LISA LAFLAMME:

When you signed up for the military did you have any clue?

NICHOLA:

No, I got to say. I signed up to go to university. I needed a job. I had no money. Somewhere along the way I fell in love with it. I'm probably a lifer now. So it's just the way it is.

LISA LAFLAMME:

So you got a university education and an all-expense – paid trip to sunny Afghanistan. Describe your job.

NICHOLA:

I'm a forward observation officer. Within the artillery, our job is to call in indirect fire. I also coordinate any fast air, whether it's jets that are going to drop bombs or do over flights. I also do link ups with the Apaches.

LISA LAFLAMME:

Give a progress report after 4 days.

NICHOLA:

I'd say it's going really well. It's easy to feel useful, going into the villages and doing the leader engagement, especially when things go well. We just report local village activity. We thought we saw a couple of guys carrying weapons but they weren't. It turned out to be umbrellas. It was disappointing. Overall, it's awesome to be here doing our job.

LISA LAFLAMME:

Do you feel the threats?

NICHOLA:

Yes. You look out for the dodgy areas so when you are going through and there are high mountains on either side, you look to see if there is anyone up there. When we go into the villages, it depends on the local response. For example, a couple of villages we went into was great – the kids came out playing and it's good. Then you go to some others and there's no one. It's 3km long and you don't see anybody. That definitely gets the hairs on the back of your neck standing up because you know they are somewhere.

LISA LAFLAMME:

How are you holding up personally?

NICHOLA:

Oh, good. It's awesome. We're sleeping far more here compared to training so right now we're really happy. I guess it just goes to show the training program prepares you and it definitely did. The real difference is the little stuff. You always make sure your rifle is where you want it. We sleep with our boots on in case we have to get up right away. Stuff like that we wouldn't do back in Canada necessarily.

The End

Nichola phoned us late in the evening of May 15th. She was at the base in Kandahar. She explained that she wouldn't be near a phone for the next little while so she wanted to wish her Dad a happy birthday. She could never tell us exactly where she was going for security reasons. She talked about how hot it was on the base, and how she slept better outside the wire. We said good night and told her to stay safe and then we hung up.

On the morning of May 17th, Tim opened his gifts and decided that he would stay at home for a little while and read the latest Leonard Cohen book I had given him. He had a meeting at 11:00 am and would make his way to the university for that. I was doing research at a school out in the northeast corner of Calgary and Kate, our youngest, was in Grade 11 at William Aberhart High School. Victoria, Nichola's other sister, was travelling in Europe.

Tim got the message a little after 10:00 am from Nichola's husband that she had been killed. No details were available as the firefight was still going on. Tim sprang into action as it was only a matter of time before the news got hold of the story. He picked up Kate, found me, and contacted Victoria. Luckily, she had reached her grandmother's house in Wales.

Over time, we pieced together what had happened. Nichola 's LAV had spent the day locating and firing on the Taliban. On May 17th, for the first time since the Korean War, she had coordinated artillery and air fire against the enemy. The battle in the Panjway district went on for most of the day.

As they retreated for the day, Nichola's head was out of the turret as she looked for the enemy. Suddenly, the enemy launched a rocket propelled grenade against the LAV, and a piece of shrapnel hit Nichola on the back of the neck, killing her instantly. Her second in command immediately sent the message to Headquarters, "My Sunray's down."

Coming Home

On May 19, there was a ramp ceremony for Nichola at the Kandahar Air Base. Troops from the NATO alliance lined the runway as her coffin was loaded onto a Hercules aircraft carrier, accompanied by one member of her battalion. Nichola's body returned to Canada on May 20, arriving at CFB Trenton after midnight.

We met the plane and watched while the coffin was loaded into the hearse. It was part of a procession of cars that left the base to return to Toronto. There, everyone would connect to Calgary flights. In those early days of the Afghan conflict, the Highway of Heroes tradition had not yet started, but even as late as it was, people lined the route outside the base, waving Canadian flags.

Epilogue
The Legacy

In the week that followed Nichola's death, a letter arrived from her, written on her 26th birthday, just over two weeks before she died.

2 May 2006

Dear Mum and Dad,

The days seem to move along at their own pace. Some days fly by, and others creep along. We are officially at the half-way point now, though. I can't believe that I've been here for 3 months. In some ways, it feels like I've been here forever. In others, as if I just got here. I am sort of getting used to things, I guess. I try to remind myself to appreciate every experience – even the ones I don't really enjoy :)

I have been thinking a lot about fate lately. It was such an accident of birth that we ended up where we did when we did. That we are where we are now, with the choices that we have available to us. It seems to me that we have such a burden of responsibility to make the world a better place for those who were born into far worse circumstances. It is more than donating money to charities – it is taking action and trying to make things better. You have both shown me that throughout my life – but here, I realize it more than ever before.

My current job and role in Afghanistan is part of that – but it is more the non-governmental organizations that come later. They are the ones that really make the difference. I like to think that my being here means they will be able to come that much sooner, and operate more freely. I will be looking for more opportunities to volunteer in Wainwright and to really try to make a difference. It is very humbling to be here, part of something so much bigger than myself.

Love always,

Nichola

I like this letter because it allows all of us to understand what motivated Nichola and in a sense, give us permission to keep going with projects that will make the world, or a little corner of it, a better place.

Nichola and her father never really agreed on the necessity of war. Tim argued that education was the key to change. Nichola told him, "You can't do that when the bad guys run things, Dad", she said, "they just shoot you. You have to have peace and good government in order for the rest to happen. I do what I do so you can do what you do."

For Tim, the opportunity to become involved in a teacher education project in Afghanistan, meant that Nichola's work and the work of all Canadian soldiers has not been in vain. He has made numerous trips to Kabul in the last five years. He believes that what the Canadians did in the years they were in Afghanistan allowed projects like his to happen.

Nichola is buried in The National War Cemetery in Beechwood. In case you haven't been there, I would recommend a visit. It really is a living memorial to our fallen. I think friends and soldiers go out there to visit and to remember. We go there every time we are in Ottawa.

On one visit, I saw two wrist bands from the 'Soldier On' organization on Nichola's grave. Another time, there was a Canadian flag, and there were roses. A couple of headstones away, another soldier from the Black Watch killed in Afghanistan was left 1/3 of a bottle of whiskey. I like to think of some of his comrades gathered for a drink and a chat, and left him his share. Just before Christmas a group goes out and places wreaths on all the headstones. At Remembrance Day, there are always poppies. Once, I met one of the full time gardeners who work there and she explained that they leave the flowers and items for a little while and then they clean them up. But more keep coming.

The end of Nichola's life has been the beginning of a new chapter in our lives. Tim and I began the Nichola Goddard Foundation which funds scholarships and solar lights in rural health centres in Papua New Guinea. We continue to raise money for projects we feel Nichola would have liked.

There have been a number of other tributes

from people from across the country who were touched by her life and her death. Since Nichola's death, numerous events and honours have happened.

In November 2006, her colleagues at CFB Shilo dedicated a trig marker on the base to Nichola. A trig marker is a survey point that fixes one's location and orientation and is used for navigation. Trig Goddard serves as a constant reminder of Nichola's sacrifice.

Nichola was awarded the Meritorious Service Medal on October 27, 2006 by the Governor General of Canada, recognizing her exemplary service in Afghanistan from January 2006 until her death on May 17, 2006. Because of this honour, MSM is written after her name.

On February 10, 2011, the government announced that one of the nine mid-shore patrol vessels in the Hero class would be named the Canadian Coast Guard Ship Captain Goddard MSM. She was built in the Halifax Shipyard and launched on May 21, 2014. Her home port is in Prince Rupert, British Columbia.

On May 2, 2013 the Calgary Board of Education officially opened the Captain Nichola Goddard middle school in Calgary. The name was chosen by the people in the community of Panorama.

Valour Canada produced a video about Nichola as part of their Monumental Canadian series. (http://www.canadianvalour.ca/heroes/nichola-goddard/videos/nichola-goddard-extended-video/).

On Remembrance Day 2012, CBC aired a documentary about Nichola, called "In the Words of a Soldier" (http://www.cbc.ca/player/play/2303123428).

In February 2015, a previously unnamed lake in northern Saskatchewan was named Goddard Lake through the GeoMemorial Program, which recognizes the sacrifices of individuals who were born or spent time in Saskatchewan and gave their lives in service.

The Goddard Peace Summit for Students is named after Nichola at East St Margaret's Bay School and has been held annually for Grade 6 students in the area since 2007.

An organ was dedicated in Nichola's memory at St. Luke's Cathedral, Sault Ste Marie, Ontario.

There is also a playground in her name in the same city outside the former Etienne Brule elementary school.

St. Jean's School, Charlottetown, dedicated their playground to her memory.

Captain Nichola Goddard's name was etched on the Memorial Arch at the Royal Military College, in Kingston, Ontario.

The Captain Nichola Goddard Memorial Sword is presented annually to the best Regular Officer Training Plan artillery senior cadet at the Royal Military College in Kingston to carry in their fourth year.

There is a Captain Nichola K.S. Goddard Memoral Scholarship at the University of Calgary

There is also a Captain Nichola K.S. Goddard Scholarship at the University of Prince Edward Island.

The Captain Nichola Goddard Memorial Trophy is awarded to the top Canadian Forces (CF) Women's Soccer Team performing in the CF regional tournament.

Nichola's death inspired the Canadian Band The Trews to write a song, 'Highway of Heroes'.

Master Corporal Jeff McCarthy of the Black Watch composed a bagpipe song entitled "Lament for Captain Goddard."

A tree was planted in her name in Fish Creek Provincial Park in Calgary, Alberta.

A gun ring in the Rogers Pass was named for her.

In October 2014, a time capsule about Nichola was placed in Beaconsfield's Heroes Park in Montreal, Quebec.

In 2017, the True Patriot Love Foundation and Canso Investment Counsel will dedicate a bridge over Highway 401, 'the Highway of Heroes', near Cobourg, Ontario to Nichola.

These legacies of Nichola extend from sea to sea to sea.

And that's why I decided to call the book 'Canada's Daughter'.

50991466R00120

Made in the USA
Middletown, DE
06 November 2017